THE POCKET GUIDEBOOK

MELBOURNE

Stephen Townshend

Little Hills Press

© Stephen Townshend, November 1997
© Photographs, Darren Hopton, 1997
Cover by NB Design
Maps by MAPgraphics.
© Maps, Little Hills Press 1997
Train and tram network reproduced with the kind permission of the
Public Transport Corporation.

Printed in Singapore
ISBN 186315 090 0

Little Hills Press Pty Ltd (ACN 002 648 393)
Regent House
37-43 Alexander Street
Crows Nest NSW 2065
Australia

DISCLAIMER
Whilst all care has been taken by the publisher and author to ensure that
the information is accurate and up to date, the publisher does not take
responsibility for the information published herein. The
recommendations are those of the author, and as things get better or
worse, places close and others open, some elements in the book may be
inaccurate when you get there. Please write and tell us about it so we can
update in subsequent edition.

Little Hills and ![trademark] are registered trademarks of
Little Hills Press Pty Ltd.

Front Cover: The dome, the Shot Tower in the futuristic
Melbourne Central shopping complex.

Back Cover: Shoppers and sculptures intermingle along
Swanston Street.

Opposite Title Page: Towers of the vertiginous dominate
Melbourne's CBD.

Contents

Introduction

Brief

Melbourne, the capital city of Victoria, lies at the mouth of the dun-coloured Yarra River. Hymned as the Garden City (Victoria, by way of symmetry, is known as the Garden State) because of its multitude of manicured parks, it is also home to great vestiges of pristine Victorian architecture and a people - at turns wowseristic and fustian but always optimistic - justly proud of the city in which they live.

Despite the indulgences of an increasingly conservative government, Melbourne remains one of the most stimulating and gracious cities in the world: couples perambulating the citys kempt and wide open streets; trams rattling past an exasperating number of heritage spots; cafés filled with people drinking macchiato and monologuing on the football; exuberant festivals in magnificently appointed venues; and markets alive with the colour of chillies, cucumbers, radichio & red peppers.

Orientation

Melbournes distinguishing mark is the flatness of its topography which means there are no natural landmarks from which to look up to or down from. Its other feature is a large and uninteresting suburbia which extends around Port Phillip Bay, into the plains to the east and west and out to the lower slopes of the Dandenong Ranges.

The city centre, laid out in a main grid by the surveyors Hoddle and Russell in 1837, squats on the northern banks of the Yarra River about five kilometres from the bay. Constant urban renewal - courtesy of the governments Agenda 21 Major Projects - has meant many public institutions have been restored and new ones created. The results, judging from Melbourne scooping the Federal Governments inaugural Australia Award for Urban Design in 1996, seem to have invigorated the city but such bravura development has hardly been met with widespread approval. Whatever your opinion of the recent Metropolis-like arrivals, the city is easy to navigate and has a reasonably good public transport system.

The main drags are Swanston Street (until recently it was the Swanston Street Walk but the appellation 'Walk was dropped when the introduction of limited after-hours traffic became a possibility) running north-south, Bourke Street and Collins Street (both running east-west). Further north and west are the former suburbs of the great unwashed while south of the Yarra River lay the slick-walled homes of the affluent.

Climate

Melbournes climate, reputedly a tonic for early immigrants suffering from tuberculosis, is variable, mostly dry and deciduous. Summers are generally skin-peelingly hot though prone to sharp changes in temperature due to Melbournes latitude and position on an 'atmospheric pressure highway. (This is why many visitors complain that the city goes in and out of season in a day.) Some respite is provided by the cooling sea breezes of Port Phillip Bay which also tend to lift temperatures in winter.

For the city as a whole, the hottest months are January and February when the average maximum temperature hovers around 26 degrees centigrade though some spells are consistently above 35 degrees centigrade. The coldest month is July when the average maximum temperature is a bracing 14 degrees centigrade. Melbourne experiences an average of 143 days of rain a year. Its rainfall, which is almost half that of Sydney, is evenly distributed with an annual average of 660mm.

Weekends, for some unfathomable reason and contrary to public perception, are drier than weekdays.

People

Melbourne's population of 3,200,000 makes it Australias second largest city after Sydney. Its continentalism - the city is home to cultures from some 60 countries including

British, Italian, Jewish, German, Greek (Melbourne has the third largest population of Greeks of any city in the world after Athens and Salonika), Maltese, Chinese and Vietnamese speaking over 70 languages - makes Melbourne one of the most cosmopolitan areas in the country. Almost half of the citys ethnic mix currently has at least one parent born overseas.

The denizens of Melbourne (known as Melburnians) have historically been characterised as an urbane, aristocratic and intellectual lot, the natural heirs to both Australia's conservative and leftist scholastic traditions, active in the arts, obsessive gardeners and sports followers, given to the notion of European decency and good living. But scratch a little deeper and you find that most Melburnians prefer the simpler things of life such as staying at home, fixatedly discussing the weather, hosting dinner parties, watching videos and fixing the back porch. Even though Melburnians may not venture out to many nightclubs or galleries they love playing in parks and dining out in restaurants.

History

Melbourne's Founding

Melbourne was established in June 1835 after John Batman, a landowner and agent of the Tasmanian-based Port Phillip Association, sailed to the mainland seeking new grazing pasturage. Batman arrived at Port Phillip where, delighted by the grassy plains and good soils, he 'purchased about 600,000 acres of land from the local Aboriginal Dutigalla people in exchange for blankets, tomahawks and assorted trinkets. Two days later he found 'the place for a village on the Yarra River ('Yarra means 'falling or free flowing, an apparent misnomer as it is neither) then sailed for Tasmania to have his claims officially recognised. John Pascoe Fawkner, another enterprising Tasmanian and jack-of-all-trades, caught wind of the fertile land on Batmans return. He hurriedly formed a small expedition which sailed up the Yarra River on the schooner *Enterprise* in August of the same year. With John Lancey at the helm, the party selected a suitable site, landed their stock and provisions, and began permanent settlement.

Although Batmans 'treaty with the Aborigines was later vetoed, settlement at Port Phillip proceeded apace, and in 1836 the settlements status was officially conferred (although it was known as the Port Phillip District of New South Wales). A year later - at the time of Queen Victoria's ascension to the throne - it was named Melbourne after Lord Melbourne (1779-1843), the then British Prime Minister.

Prosperity and Separation

Melbourne soon flourished on the back of wool and land sales, while its declaration as a free port in 1840 attracted an influx of newcomers and their families. (It was during this period that the Aboriginal population rapidly declined as it succumbed to European diseases, was slaughtered by white settlers for trespassing, shot for 'sport or set upon by trained dogs.) Important public buildings of brick and timber, commercial residences, hotels and footpaths were constructed with scattershot aplomb, while evolving domestic architecture - houses were built away from the sun so residents were spared the fierce, roasted and roaring hot heatwaves - spoke of the city's substantial individual wealth. Melbourne grew into a bold and adventurous metropolis and was proclaimed a city in 1847.

Melbourne's growth showed no signs of retardation and this, coupled with the vigorous self-assertiveness of its citizens, led to the city's separation from New South Wales and the proclamation of the new colony of Victoria in 1850. Gold was discovered in Victoria a year later heralding the arrival of more immigrants as well as attracting some of the world's finest architects and artisans who spurred the development of new suburbs such as St Kilda and Hawthorn. Melbourne became the 'capital of the El Dorado of the south, a boomtown of unforseen riches for some, yet a place of hardship and penury for many'.

After the deposits of gold were exhausted, Melbourne's population and confidence declined. But by the 1880s the city - buttressed by an injection of British capital and buoyed by mining and property speculation - was once again on the ascent. A flurry of conspicuous civic spending saw the creation of florid buildings, parklands and gardens in the city and surrounding suburbs. Melbourne, previously considered a coarse and jumped-up English town, was bestowed the sobriquet 'Marvellous' as it was transformed into an Antipodean equivalent of the great cities of the world. The city's vaulting ambition was further highlighted when it played host to the rest of the world at the Great Exhibition of 1880.

However Melbourne's Golden Age evaporated during the bank crash and the Depression of the 1890s. Caution and conservatism became the new traits which were to dominate the city's thinking well into the next century.

The 20th Century

By the beginning of the 20th century Melbourne had become the capital and seat of the national Parliament, a role it relinquished when these honours were transferred to Canberra in 1927. The city continued to prosper during the 1920s but any further growth was undermined by the Great Depression. Melbourne was again battered and bruised but the implementation by the government of a series of public works programs - including the building of the Shrine of Remembrance, St Kilda Road and the Great Ocean Road - significantly boosted morale.

After World War II the economy stabilised but by the 1970s Melbourne's position as Australias leading city was under threat from Sydney. The shift of power northwards continued but the election of John Cains Labor government in 1982 raised expectations of a much-needed renaissance. However it was not to be. Labor's increasing economic mismanagement, its exposure to a worsening national recession and the collapse of some of its largest financial institutions led to an overwhelming Liberal/National coalition victory in 1992.

Melbourne Today

The government, under Premier Jeff Kennett, has since strode like a colossus over the political landscape. It has revitalised the states economy; initiated a bewildering number of legislative changes and building projects (construction totalling over $3 billion is either under way or planned for in the city centre); trampled upon a divided, introspective and sullen Opposition (admittedly their cause hasn't been helped by choosing a leader whose capacity for being uninteresting amounts to genius); and won a second term with another huge majority in 1996. All this has been achieved despite the government *not* taking the public into its confidence or including them in consultation. For a city historically accustomed to breathing ideas of delicate fancy, of refining and humanising politics, such expressions of political self-interest are taking some getting used to.

Festivals and Events

Melburnians are a festive bunch with many organisations hosting a frenzied array of non-stop food and wine, music, dance, theatre, cinema, sporting and artistic happenings throughout the year. The government's strategy is to host one major event a month and so far they've succeeded staging the Formula One Grand Prix, Ford Australian Open, Australian Football League (AFL) Grand Final, Melbourne International Festival, Three Tenors, and so on.

For up-to-date information on the city's events pick up the 'What's on' listings available from tourist information offices (see the following Travel Tips chapter for their locations). Bookings to most events can be made through the BASS agency, ph 11 566 (open Monday to Saturday from 9am-9pm and Sunday from 10am-5pm), or by visiting any BASS outlet in the city (locations include Myers, Daimaru, Southgate and the Victorian Arts Centre) or suburbs.

January
The Ford Australian Open
This Grand Slam tennis championship is held over two weeks at the National Tennis Centre, Batman Avenue. The event attracts a number of top-drawer players including Pete Sampras and Martina Hingis as well as Australians Pat Rafter, Mark Phillippousis and the 'Woodies (Mark Woodforde and Mark Woodbridge), the worlds number one ranked doubles pairing.
The Summer Music Festival
The Victorian Arts Centre hosts a range of musical concerts from classics to uptempo rock.
Marvellous Melbourne Jazz Festival
This recent addition to the Melbourne jazz scene replaces the internationally renowed three-day Montsalvat International Jazz Festival. It's low-key, mostly bland fare

that promises little in the way of innovation or new talent.

February

The St Kilda Festival
A week-long contemporary arts and culture program featuring food, wine, music, art and literature, and finishing with a fireworks display over St Kilda Beach.

The Australian Matchplay and Australian Masters Golf Tournaments
These two major sporting events are held on the city's sandbelt courses which include Royal Melbourne, Huntingdale and Kingston Heath.

The Victoria Street Festival
A colourful and chaotic celebration of Vietnamese culture.

Chinese New Year
Chinatown becomes a raucous but extremely enjoyable location for a range of events such as lion dances and the awakening of the world's longest dragon.

The Melbourne Music Festival
Showcases contemporary local music at various indoor/outdoor venues throughout the city.

March

The Moomba Festival
The 10-day Moomba Festival ('Moomba is an Aboriginal word meaning 'getting together and having fun'), held annually since 1953, is a Melbourne cultural institution. Events include exhibitions, parades, fireworks displays and comic sporting contests such as the Birdman Rally.

The Antipodes Festival
Australias largest ethnic festival focuses on the rich culture and heritage of Greek Australians. Festivities culminate on 25 March which is the Greek National Day.

The Irish Festival
Expect to see actors, distinctively garbed in yesteryear attire, reciting Beckett, Joyce *et al* at various locations around the city. Theres also talent quests and the ubiquitous St Patrick's Day Parade. An official program of events is available from the Irish Shop at Daimaru, Melbourne Central and the Royal Arcade.

The Melbourne Food and Wine Festival
Melbourne immodestly celebrates its standing as the culinary capital of Australia with a number of gut-pleasing food and wine events.

Formula One Grand Prix
A four-day event of baying cars and high-octane excitement (or so the posters would have you believe). Away from the track theres a plethora of surrounding activities including street parties and grand balls. When the Grand Prix was first staged at Albert Park there was much local protest but things should be quieter now.

April

The Melbourne International Comedy Festival
Any festival that begins on April Fool's Day has to be a hoot. Held since 1986, the Melbourne International Comedy Festival currently ranks alongside the Edinburgh Fringe and Montreal's *Juste Pour Rire* as one of the best celebrations of comedy in the world.

The St Kilda Film Festival
Australian short films are to the fore in this emerging annual event.

The Melbourne International Flower and Garden Show
Another world-class event with spectacular displays of flowers and shrubbery.

May

The Next Wave Festival
Arts festival for up-and-coming professional artists. Events including art and technology displays, performance theatre, writing and visual arts, are held in venues ranging from the National Gallery through to bookshops and tiny artist-run spaces.

June

The Melbourne International Film Festival
A two-week event that is one of the worlds oldest film festivals, having run for over 40 years. Showcases the finest crop of local and international releases.

September

The Royal Melbourne Show

Held over 11 days at the Royal Melbourne Showgrounds in Flemington, this predominantly agricultural fair attracts some 800,000 visitors with activities such as stud-livestock judging, horse-riding competitions, wood-chopping contests, arts and craft displays plus rides and novelty events.

AFL Grand Final

Melbourne becomes a sea of badges, scarves and other clothing in the colours of the two football clubs battling it out on the last Saturday in September. Mementoes sold on the day become valued icons while certain players are exalted as gods. The sprawling Melbourne Cricket Ground (MCG), Australias sporting Mecca, is the centre for the homage.

October

The Melbourne International Festival

The citys artistic and cultural standout was initially established in 1986 to showcase the Victorian Arts Centre. It now runs over 17 days and features food and wine, performing and visual arts, music, theatre, dance and literature at assorted locations. Over 3000 artists participate with the highlights being the Melbourne Writers Festival and the avant-garde Melbourne Fringe Arts Festival. The latter spans 21 days and has over 230 events including abseilers scaling prominent city buildings, live theatre in the Myers department store window and 'staged scatological verbal stoushes'. It kicks off with the traditional free-for-all street party and parade in Brunswick Street, Fitzroy, and winds up with a fitting finale at Station Pier, South Melbourne.

The Caulfield Cup

This 2400m horse race, first run in 1879, is part of the Spring Racing Carnival - 29 days of galloping horse flesh, conspicuous partying and preening fashion shows notable for their silly headgear.

November

The Melbourne Cup
The most famous horse race in Australia is always run on the first Tuesday in November. First held in 1861, it is, along with the AFL Grand Final, the most eagerly anticipated sporting event in the country.

The Italian Lygon Street Festa
Lygon Street is closed to traffic then filled with foodstalls, bandstands and hawkers celebrating Melbourne's illustrious Italian heritage. The highlight of the weekend's festivities is the much-anticipated Waiters Race.

The Great Victorian Bike Race
Classic ride that runs from the Grampians to Melbourne (over 630km), passing some of the states famous natural sights including Port Fairy, the Twelve Apostles and the beautiful west-coast beaches. Its on between 30 November-8 December and the cost, which includes all meals plus luggage transport, is $333/378 for children/adults.

December

Carols by Candlelight
Over 25,000 people cram the Sidney Myer Music Bowl to be entertained by local musicians and sing Christmas carols under the stars.

Public Holidays

Melbournes public holidays are:
New Years Day - 1 January
Australia Day - held on the Monday closest to 26 January
Labour Day - second Monday in March
Easter - Good Friday and Easter Saturday, Monday and Tuesday - celebrated at the end of March or early April
Australia and New Zealand Army Corps (ANZAC) Day - 25 April
Queens Birthday - second Monday in June
Melbourne Cup Day - first Tuesday in November
Christmas Day - 25 December
Boxing Day - 26 December

Travel Tips

Airport Facilities

Melbournes comfortable and efficient Tullamarine International Airport is about 20km north-west of the city centre. The drive, which takes around 40 minutes (less outside peak-hour traffic), winds dully along the freeway through industrial estates and a patchwork of red, green and brown suburban hillsides.

Tullamarine is one of Australia's busiest airports, handling almost two million international and over seven million domestic passengers annually. Both international and domestic flights depart from the airport, and use the same terminal.

The airport has a number of facilities including baggage lockers ($4 a day) on the ground and 1st floors of the International Terminal; baggage trolleys which can be hired from the car park and departure level for $2 (free for arriving passengers in the International Baggage Reclaim Hall); currency exchanges (open 24-hours a day, seven days a week) located on the ground floor, Customs Hall, departure concourse and 1st floor of the International Terminal; a general information desk at the International Arrivals Hall plus a Travellers Information Service on the ground floor providing accommodation, transport and tour bookings; a lost property service (ph 9393 1737); a parents room for baby changing; both short and long-term carparks ($7 a day, $42 week/maximum $15 per 24-hour period); 24-hour emergency first aid; and a medical centre-cum-dental service at the Ansett end of the International Terminal ($30 for a standard consultation).

The airport also features a food court and bar on the 1st floor, specialty shops and duty-free stores, showers, valet parking, postal services, a prayer room, and a reasonably good children's playground on the departure level of the International Terminal. Taxis are available outside the terminal along the ground floor while all major rental companies have offices at the airport.

Tullamarine is currently undergoing a $192 million facelift which will further improve services and double its passenger-handling capacity.

For information on getting to/from the airport see the Getting Around chapter.

Airline Offices

International airline offices in Melbourne are:

Aerolineas Argentinas, ph 9650 7111
Air France, ph 9672 7122
Air New Zealand, ph 13 2476
Alitalia, ph 9670 0171
Ansett, ph 13 1300
British Airways, ph 9603 1133
Cathay Pacific, ph 13 1747
Garuda, ph 13 1223
Japan Airlines, ph 9654 2733
KLM, ph 9654 5222
Lufthansa, ph 9602 5144
Malaysian Airlines, ph 13 2627
Qantas, ph 13 1313
Singapore Airlines, ph 9602 4555
Thai Airways, ph 9650 5066
United Airlines, ph 13 1777

Business Hours

Business hours are generally Monday to Friday 9am-5.30pm. Banking hours are Monday to Thursday 9am-4pm, and Friday 9.30am-5pm. The government has recently relaxed shopping restrictions and its now possible to shop till you drop round-the-clock, seven days a week. General shop trading is banned only on Good Friday, Christmas Day and Anzac Day morning. Trading hours are mostly Monday to Thursday 9am-5.30pm, Friday 9am-9pm, and Saturday 9am-12.30pm (open to 5pm in the city centre). Late-night shopping in the city centre is on Thursday when stores close their doors at 9pm. Some suburban precincts and their shopping strips, such as Carlton (Lygon Street), St Kilda (Acland Street),

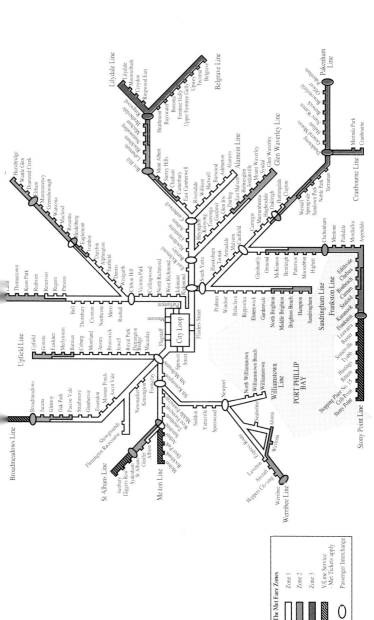

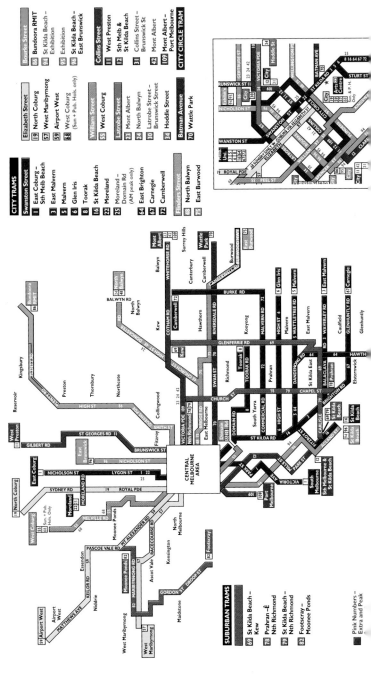

Prahran (Chapel Street) and Fitzroy (Brunswick Street), are open seven days a week.

Child Care

The following child care facilities are in the city centre:

Melbourne Central, 300 Lonsdale Street, ph 9665 0000 - open seven days a week though service is limited on the weekend.

Melbourne Occasional Care, 104 ABeckett Street, ph 9329 9561 - open Monday to Friday (no weekend service).

Churches and Temples

Most of Melbournes magnificent array of inner-city churches were built in the mid-19th century at the height of the gold-rush boom. Services are held on weekdays and Sunday (unless stated otherwise), and all are welcome.

Anglican

St Paul's Cathedral, cnr Swanston and Flinders Streets, ph 9650 3791.

St James' Old Cathedral, cnr King and Batman Streets, ph 9329 6133.

St Peter's Church, cnr Gisborne and Albert Streets, ph 9662 2391.

Baptist

Collins Street Baptist Church, 174 Collins Street, ph 9650 1180 (Sunday only).

Churches of Christ

Swanston Street Church of Christ, cnr Swanston and Little Lonsdale Streets, ph 9663 3884.

Greek Orthodox

Greek Orthodox Church (East Melbourne), 861 Victoria Parade, ph 9662 1362.

Jewish

East Melbourne Synagogue, 488 Albert Street, East Melbourne, ph 9662 1372.

Presbyterian

Scots Church, 99 Russell Street, ph 9650 9903.

Welsh Calvinist Methodist Church, 320 La Trobe Street, ph 9329 6961 (Sunday only).

Roman Catholic
St Patrick's Cathedral, cnr Albert and Gisborne Streets, ph 9662 2233.
St Francis' Church, cnr Lonsdale and Elizabeth Streets, ph 9663 2485.
St Augustine's Church, 631 Bourke Street, ph 9629 7494.
Salvation Army
Salvation Army Temple, 69 Bourke Street, ph 9653 3206.
Uniting Church
St Michael's Uniting Church, 120 Collins Street, ph 9654 5120 (Sunday only).
Wesley Uniting Church, 148 Lonsdale St, ph 9662 2355.

Communications

Mail
Melbourne's General Post Office (GPO), cnr Elizabeth and Bourke Streets, ph 9203 3044, is open Monday to Friday 8.15am-5.30pm, and Saturday 10am-1pm (for stamp service, paying bills and collecting mail only). The poste restante section is located at the rear of the building. Stamps can also be purchased in the city from Australia Post shops (at various locations), newsagents and some milk bars, as well as the National Philatelic Centre, ph 9650 3110, on the corner of Latrobe and Exhibition Streets. Suburban post offices are usually open Monday to Friday 9am-5pm.

Postage for a standard letter within Australia is 45c. The cost of air-mail letters (postcards are slightly cheaper) to the following overseas destinations are:
New Zealand, Singapore and Malaysia 75c
Hong Kong, India and Japan 95c
USA and Canada.....................................$1.05
UK and Europe...$1.20

Telephone
Public telephones are dotted around the city in hotels, shops, bars, cafés and restaurants, on specially designated sites on footpaths, as well as the GPO.

A local call from a public telephone costs 40c. The area code for Melbourne is 03.

Subscriber Trunk Dialling (STD)

Long-distance STD calls can be made from public telephones. Fees vary depending on the distance involved and the time the call is placed. If you're reluctant to carry around pockets of change, consider buying a phonecard (eg Telstra Phoneaway, Telstra Telecard, Optus Calling Card or Satellite Cowboys World Axxess). These come in a range of denominations from $2-$100, and can be used from hotel rooms, hostels, and public pay phones both locally and overseas. The phonecards, often featuring typical Australian landscapes, are available at airport, duty-free and souvenir stores, Telstra shops, selected travel agents and major newsagents. They're light, extremely handy and can be used repeatedly until the cards value has expired.

International Subscriber Dialling (ISD)

Overseas calls can be made by dialling ISD. Simply ring 0011 (the overseas access code), followed by the country code, area code and then the required telephone number. The cheapest time to call overseas is at night and on weekends, especially between 11pm and 6am on Sunday.

For information on country and area codes, off-peak charges and time zones, refer to the back of the White Pages of the Melbourne Telephone Directory.

Country Direct

This service enables travellers direct access (for the price of a local call) to operators in their home country to make credit card or reverse charge (collect) calls. Countries involved with this service are found in the White Pages A-K (Telstra clients) and White Pages L-Z (Optus clients).

Telephone Interpreter Service

This is a free service operating 24 hours a day. Assistance in over 100 languages is offered by calling 13 1450.

Fax

Faxes can be sent from any Melbourne post office, major newsagents and chemists, and specialist businesses such as photocopying shops. Faxes sent from a post office to a destination within Australia cost $4/1 for the first page/subsequent pages while overseas faxes are $10/4.

Time Zones
Because of its vast size Australia is made up of the following three time zones:
Eastern Standard Time (Victoria, New South Wales, Queensland and Tasmania) - 10 hours ahead of Greenwich Mean Time (GMT/UTC).
Central Time (South Australia and the Northern Territory) - nine and a half hours ahead of GMT/UTC.
Western Standard Time (West Australia) - eight hours ahead of GMT/UTC.

Melbourne (and Victoria) operates on daylight-saving time when clocks are put forward one hour at 2am on the last Sunday in October and remain so until the last Sunday in March.

Useful Telephone Numbers
Some useful numbers include:

Emergencies (free call) - 000 for 24-hour operator assistance (the operator can then connect you to police, ambulance or fire brigade services)

Directory Assistance (free call) - 013 for a local number, 0175 for a country and interstate number, 0103 for an overseas number

Reverse Charges (domestic) - 0176 from a public payphone, 011 from a private telephone

Reverse Charges (international) - 0107 from a public payphone, 0101 from a private telephone

Calling Difficulties (calls within Australia) - 1100

Calling Difficulties (calls overseas) - 0100

Weather - 1196

Consulates

Melbournes foreign consulates include:

Austria, 897 High Street, Armadale, ph 9509 0360

Canada, 123 Camberwell Road, Hawthorn East, ph 9811 9999

China, 77 Irving Road, Toorak, ph 9822 0604

Denmark, 7 Acacia Avenue, Blackburn, ph 9894 1383

Germany, 480 Punt Road, South Yarra, ph 9828 6888
France, 492 St Kilda Road, Melbourne, ph 9820 0921
Greece, 34 Queens Road, Melbourne, ph 9866 4524
Hungary, 115 Collins Street, Melbourne, ph 9650 8636
Indonesia, 72 Queens Road, Melbourne, ph 9525 2755
Italy, 509 St Kilda Road, Melbourne, ph 9867 5744
Japan, 360 Elizabeth Street, Melbourne, ph 9639 3244
Malaysia, 492 St Kilda Road, Melbourne, ph 9867 5339
New Zealand, 60 Albert Road, South Melbourne,
ph 9696 0399
Norway, 31st Floor, 120 Collins Street, Melbourne,
ph 9654 8020
Spain, 766 Elizabeth Street, Melbourne, ph 9347 1966
Sweden, 61 Riggall St, Broadmeadows, ph 9301 1888
Switzerland, 420 St Kilda Rd, Melbourne, ph 9867 2266
Thailand, 277 Flinders Lane, Melbourne, ph 9650 1714
UK, 17th Floor, 90 Collins St, Melbourne, ph 9650 4155
USA, 553 St Kilda Road, Melbourne, ph 9526 5900

Electricity

Electricity supply throughout Australia is 220-240V, AC
50 cycles. Three-pronged plugs are the norm meaning AC
110V appliances, such as hairdryers, require transformers.
Fortunately most hotels, hardware stores and chemists
supply adaptor plugs.

Entry Formalities

All travellers to Australia require a valid passport and
visa (New Zealanders are the only nationality exempt
from the latter). Tourist visas are available from
Australian embassies, consular offices, high commissions
and travel agents, and are usually valid for either three or
six-month stays.

Travellers are allowed to bring into Australia duty-free
goods to the value of $A400 plus one litre of alcohol and
250 cigarettes. It is prohibited to carry into the country
narcotics (unless accompanied by a prescription),
weaponry (unless with a permit), products derived from
protected wildlife species, and live animals and/or birds.
Customs officials are also wary of goods made from

animal or vegetable matter (wooden carvings, straw baskets and the like), meat, fruit and vegetables. You should declare all such items on arrival otherwise they may be confiscated or open to fine.

Exit Formalities

A departure tax of $27 is required for everyone over the age of 12 years leaving the country by air. This is built into the price of the ticket, so it is no longer necessary to purchase stamps.

Health

Melbourne is as safe a destination as you could possibly imagine. Your main health risks are likely to be from sunburn, foot blisters, upset stomachs through overeating and drinking, and hot, irritable flushes bought on by Premier Kennett's hare-brained outbursts. Medical care is excellent and consultations are reasonably cheap ($30-40). And to top it all off, you can drink as much tap water as you like - its among the cleanest and tastiest drinking water in the world.

Medical services for the traveller include:

Travellers Medical Clinic, Level 2, 393 Little Bourke Street, ph 9602 5788 - excellent traveller service with specially trained doctors and nurses, vaccinations a specialty, standard consultation is $35, opening hours are variable but generally 9am-5pm (open Monday, Tuesday and Thursday until 9pm). However, you can call into any doctor's surgery for treatment, just clarify the cost beforehand.

Information

Tourist Offices

The city centre is endowed with excellent sources of information. Both *Tourism Victoria*, Melbourne Town Hall, Swanston Street, ph 9650 1522, and *Information Victoria*, 356 Collins Street, ph 9651 4100, are chock full of brochures and travel-related information, and can book tours and accommodation for Melbourne and country Victoria, as well as interstate.

The city council also has three information booths at the following locations:

Bourke Street Mall - open Monday to Friday from 9am-5pm, Saturday from 10am-4pm, Sunday from 11am-4pm

Collins Street (City Square) - open the same hours as the Bourke Street Mall information booth

Rialto Towers - open Monday to Friday 11am-5pm, and weekends 10am-4pm.

Media

Newspapers

Melbournes two daily newspapers are *The Age* (90c on weekdays, $1.30 on weekends) and *Herald Sun* (70c on weekdays, $1.20 on weekends). *The Age*, a once formidable and respected liberal broadsheet now fallen on hard times, features the odd good reportage on corporate, political and social issues, occasional exposés on government ratbaggery, supplements on the arts and fine dining, and a sports section unhealthily preoccupied with Australian Rules. In completely the opposite vein is the higher-circulation, *Herald-Sun*. Unashamedly tabloid in style, it devotes much of its pages to sex, mass murderers, killer dogs and dodgy welfare cheats, and boasts an even unhealthier preoccupation with Australian Rules. Both are available at newsagents, newspaper kiosks/stands scattered around the city centre, milk bars, delis, and some chemists. Newspapers are also available to be read at public libraries and some inner-city cafés and restaurants.

Two national dailies - the Sydney dominated, Rupert Murdoch-owned *Australian* (90c on weekdays, $1.20 on Saturday) and the business-minded *Australian Financial Review* ($1.50 on weekdays) - as well as various international and foreign-language publications are also available throughout the city.

Radio

Melbournes radio stations include:

AM

Radio National (621) - all ages audience, a government-funded Australian Broadcasting Corporation (ABC)

station featuring the cream of the country's radio talent (Peter Thompson, Norman Swan, Louise Adler, Geraldine Doogue, Robin Williams and Phillip Adams), excellent local and national news coverage, business, the arts, educational and special interest topics, heavily criticised by some as too left-leaning.

Magic (693) - 40 to 60-plus audience, golden oldies hits.

3LO (774) - 40 to 60-plus audience, ABC station featuring plenty of talkback, reasonably penetrating interviews, good news service.

3CR (855) - all ages audience, community radio station, multicultural programs.

Sport 927 (927) - predominantly 50-plus male audience, acres of Australian Rules and racing coverage, gossipy format, formerly 3UZ.

3SBS (1224) - all ages audience, foreign-language and world music programs.

3AW (1278) - 40 to 60-plus audience, tabloid radio that consistently outrates other stations in Melbourne, home of some of the city's most overblown personalities including talkback king Neil Mitchell, the Coodabeens, Sam Newman, Rex Hunt and Ernie Sigley, minuscule guest interviews but in-depth weekend football broadcasts.

FM

3ZZZ (92.3) - all ages audience, community ethnic radio station. 3SBS (93.1) - all ages audience, foreign-language programs.

FOXFM (101.9) - contemporary audience, consistently second to 3AW in the ratings, some talented hosts including the hilarious Martin & Molloy in the drive slot.

3RRR (102.7) - contemporary audience, community radio station, excellent alternative music, lively talkback.

3MBS (103.5) - 40 to 60-plus audience, mostly classics.

3MMM (105.1) - contemporary audience, middle-of -the-road rock.

ABC Classic FM (105.9) - 40 to 60-plus audience, ABC station with good interviews and hosts including Margaret Throsby, interviews, classical music, reasonable news coverage.

3PBS (106.7) - contemporary audience, community radio station, alternative/independent music with a heavy slant on techno and trance, some current affairs and comedy.

Triple J (107.5) - contemporary audience, ABC station targeting the nations 'youth, alternative/independent' music, mostly predictable talkback discussing 'right-on' issues, hosts include Francis Leach, 'Calamity Jane and the popular but hit-and-miss breakfast team of Mikey Robbins and Paul McDermott.

Television

Melbournes television channels are:

ABC2 (Channel Two) - distinctively Australian national broadcaster, commercial-free, good coverage of sport, drama, comedy (look out for *Frontline*, a side-splittingly funny send-up of television news), current affairs and the arts, though recent budget cuts forced by the Federal Government has meant the axing of a large chunk of local programming.

HSV7 (Channel Seven) - commercial network featuring the best local and overseas drama, some great comedy, extensive sports coverage including live Australian Rules matches, reliable movies.

GTV9 (Channel Nine) - commercial network, No 1 in the ratings, surprisingly lacklustre sports coverage although rugby league is telecast live during the season, execrable infotainment shows, blockbuster movies.

TEN10 (Channel 10) - commercial network, great overseas imports including *The Simpsons*, *Seinfield*, *Melrose Place* and *The X Files*, patchy movies.

Special Broadcasting Service (SBS) (Channel 28) - Australia's multicultural broadcaster, foreign-language, in-depth current affairs and special interest features, good coverage of international sport especially soccer, excellent world and classic cinema, the best mid-evening news of all the channels.

Literature

Melbourne has long produced writers of the first rank. These number the sometimes controversial Helen Garner (*Monkey Grip*, *Cosmo Cosmolina*, *the first stone*), Booker Prize winner Peter Carey (*Illywhacker*, *Oscar and Lucinda*, *The Tax Inspector*) as well as an emerging group of literary tyros headed by Christos Tsiolkas, Eric Dando, Virginia Trioli and Delia Faulkner. Works by these authors are available at most Melbourne bookshops (see Shopping chapter for the locations of city and suburban bookshops).

Film

The filmography of Melbourne is uniformly vast. Movies made about the city and its citizenry hark back to 1900 but more recent efforts include the whimsical *Malcolm* and *The Big Steal*, both shot by the husband and wife team of Nadia Tass and David Parker, Mark Joffes *Spotswood*, a sentimental slice of postwar Melbourne starring Anthony Hopkins, and Jocelyn Moorhouses *Proof*, an unsettling and ironic film about a blind man with an obsessive predilection for photography.

Other quintessential Melburnian films are: Geoffrey Wright's *Romper Stomper* (a gritty *tour de force* that traces the pathetic and brutal lives of a group of Footscray skinheads) and *Metal Skin* (more urban alienation though this time skinheads have been replaced by car hoons); Richard Lowenstein's *Dogs in Space* (drugs, punk rock and INXS lead singer Michael Hutchence); John Ruane's *Death in Brunswick* (sardonic goings-on in inner Melbourne); Richard Franklin's *Hotel Sorrento* (a rather cloying slice of sisterly relationships); John Tatouli's *The Silver Brumby* (high-country adventure); and anything by the idiosyncratic director Paul Cox (*Lonely Hearts*, *A Womans Tale*, *Man of Flowers* and the very successful *Lust and Revenge*).

More contemporary films include Michael Rymer's much-hyped *Angel Baby*, a rather implausible though deeply moving story of two schizophrenics, Emma-Kate Groghan's hilarious *Love and Other Catastrophes*, a low-budget debut feature (it was shot for only A\$45,000 in under 17 days) about student romance that delighted audiences in Cannes as well as critics at home, and Craig Rosenberg's *Hotel de Love*, a romantic saga about two fraternal twins falling for the same girl. If you get the chance, try and also catch *Bitter Herbs and Honey*. This warm and intelligent documentary by Monique Schwarz imaginatively details the lives of Carlton's Jewish families through the years.

Most of the preceding films are available for hire at video outlets.

Money

Australia has a decimal currency system where 100 cents equals one dollar. Notes come in denominations of $5, $10, $20, $50 and $100, and coins in 5c, 10c, 20c, 50c, $1 and $2.

Most banks and some of the larger hotels can change travellers cheques (American Express, Thomas Cook, Visa, etc) or foreign currency. There are also several foreign exchange branches located in the city including Thomas Cook, 257 Collins Street, ph 9650 2442 and 330 Collins Street, ph 9602 3811, as well as American Express, 233 Collins Street, ph 9633 6333.

Credit Cards

Major credit cards such as *American Express*, *Diners Club*, *Visa* and *MasterCard* are widely accepted in Australia. Credit cards can also be used to obtain cash advances from banks. Retail outlets, cafés and restaurants regularly display the logos of accepted cards on their front doors or at check-out counters.

Tipping

Tipping is not compulsory in Australia (even though some in the hospitality industry think otherwise). However, if you've been impressed by particularly good service at a hotel, restaurant or from a taxi driver, leaving a tip is certainly not frowned upon. Generally any tip around 10% of the bill is much appreciated.

Travellers with Disabilities

The Met has a number of services available to passengers with special needs. These include the Disability Services Department (ph 9619 2355), facilities for customers with hearing and speech impairments (ph 9619 2727), and a wheelchair accessible minibus for the St Kilda and Port Melbourne area (ph 008 012 061, toll free).

A good publication to get hold of is the *Mobility Map of Central Melbourne*. Copies provide information on accessible routes and toilets in the city, locations of street ramps, multi-access public telephones, 'disabled parking bays', and buildings with steep gradients. The map can be obtained from the front desk of the Melbourne Town Hall, Swanston Street, ph 9658 9763.

Other organisations providing information and services for the disabled include:

Travellers' Aid Society of Victoria, 169 Swanston Street, ph 9654 2600 - accessible showers and lockers, recreational lounge, excellent support centre (ph 9654 7690), there is another branch at the Spencer Street Station, ph 9670 2873.

Helping Hand (various locations throughout the city), ph 9619 2300 - offers assistance to country and interstate train travellers, provides wheelchairs and help at stations, bookings are necessary.

Melbourne's Disability Services Unit, ph 9616 7777 - a government organisation which has built wheelchair ramps on trains, tactile tiles for the visually impaired as well as hearing induction loops, special grab rails and high-visibility edging strips at train stations.

Weights and Measures

Australia uses the metric system. Distances are measured in kilometres, weights in kilograms, temperatures in degrees Celsius, liquids in litres, and so on.

Accommodation

Both Melbourne's skyscrapered city centre and surrounding suburbs hold a wealth of accommodation options. You can choose from upmarket hotels, the rather cloyingly termed 'boutique hotels', serviced apartments, motels, bed and breakfasts (B&Bs), pubs, hostels and guesthouses. There are generally plenty of rooms available throughout the year but if you plan a visit during the Spring Racing Carnival, the AFL Grand Final or the Formula One Grand Prix be sure to book ahead.

Prices quoted in this chapter are for standard single and double rooms mid-week (unless stated otherwise). Most of the following upmarket and mid-range hotels also offer corporate rates.

City Centre
Upmarket Hotels
Sheraton Towers Southgate, 1 Brown Street, ph 9696 3100 - good location in the hub of the city's arts and cultural precinct, elegant Victorian furnishings, health club, heated pool - from $345.

Grand Hyatt Melbourne, 123 Collins Street, ph 9657 1234 - massive hotel with over 547 rooms and 18 executive suites, the haunt of the rich, retired and recognised, good location, great views over the city from the top floors, excellent service (butlers on call), good theatre packages available, facilities include gymnasium, tennis court, sauna and spa, heated indoor pool - from $330.

Crown Towers Hotel, Crown Casino, Level 2, 99 Queensbridge Street, ph 9292 6666 - 500-room hotel that is part of the gigantic Crown Casino complex, very swish, excellent package deals - from $295.

Le Meridien at Rialto Melbourne, 495 Collins Street, ph 9620 9111 - all 19th-century Venetian spires, towering glass-roofed atrium, swish bars and brasserie, spa and sauna, heated rooftop pool - from $250.

Hotel Sofitel, 25 Collins Street, ph 9653 0000 - 363 rooms, typically luxurious accommodation and services, great views, the hotel is closely aligned with the arts which is reflected in a range of exhibitions held on-site throughout the year, discounts rates apply according to availability, formerly The Regent Melbourne - from $240.

The Sebel of Melbourne, 321 Flinders Lane, ph 9629 4088 - small and luxurious hotel, considerable character, private courtyard garden, conference facilities - from $240.

The Windsor, 103 Spring Street, ph 9653 0653 - sumptuous and elegant building that is Australia's last remaining grand deluxe hotel, built in the late 19th century and classified by the National Trust, features superb interior furnishings that have been lovingly restored. Great service, good restaurants and fantastic location at the 'top end' of the city - from $225.

Rockmans Regency Hotel, cnr Exhibition and Lonsdale Streets, ph 9662 3900 - small and very private luxury hotel, solarium, sauna and spa, pool - from $219.

Mid-Range Hotels

Adelphi Hotel, 187 Flinders Lane, ph 9650 7555 - 34 rooms, located in the heart of the city, opened in 1992, designed by the famed architectural firm Denton Corker Marshall (DCM), modernist decor with sleekly functional couches and brightly coloured tables and chairs, minimal rooms with spacious bathrooms, excellent bars and restaurants, great views, 24-hour news service, gymnasium, spa, 25-metre lap pool (a Melbourne landmark) that overhangs the street below - from $210.

Centra Melbourne on the Yarra, cnr Flinders and Spencer Streets, ph 9629 5111 - close to casino and public transport - from $180.

Novotel Melbourne on Collins, 270 Collins Street, ph 9650 5800 - 323 rooms, good location buried among the ritzy Australia-on-Collins shopping complex, reasonable brasserie, gymnasium, sauna and spa, indoor heated swimming pool - from $169.

Savoy Park Plaza International, 630 Little Collins Street, ph 9622 8888 - 1920s era hotel, charming interior, good service - from $165.

Banks Hotel, cnr Flinders Lane and Spencer Street, ph 9629 4111 - good location and services - from $160.

Ibis Hotel Melbourne, 15 Therry Street, ph 9639 2399 - 250 fully equipped and comfortable rooms, restaurant and bar, conference facilities, gym - from $135.

Batmans Hill Hotel, 66 Spencer Street, ph 9614 6344 - has character and charm, recently restored, good food, price includes breakfast and welcome drink - from $130.

The Sheraton Hotel Melbourne, 13 Spring Street, ph 9205 9999 - close walking distance to the city's gardens, sights and nightspots, price includes breakfast - from $115.

Hotel Grand Chancellor, 131 Lonsdale Street, ph 9663 3161 - located in the heart of the city's theatre district (offers accommodation and theatre packages), easy walking distance to Chinatown, recently renovated, reasonable restaurants and bars, conference facilities, sauna, heated swimming pool, formerly the New Chateau Hotel - from $105.

Standard Hotels

Terrace Pacific Inn, 16 Spencer Street, ph 9621 3333 - close to public transport, restaurants, nightclubs and shops, walking distance to the casino and World Congress Centre, above average bar and bistro, conference facilities, price includes breakfast - from $99.

Hotel Enterprize, 44 Spencer Street, ph 9629 6991 - near casino, lacklustre restaurant - from $89.

The Hotel Y, 489 Elizabeth Street, ph 9329 5188 - recently refurbished and now boasts a dramatic and head-turning frontage, expressive verandah that juts over the street, simple but comfortable budget rooms to 3-star business-style apartments, conference facilities, fitness and recreation centre, good wholesome food in ground floor café, heated indoor pool, formerly the YWCA - dorms from $23, singles/doubles from $60.

Kingsgate Hotel, 131 King Street, ph 9629 4171 - good budget accommodation, close to public transport, 24-hour reception, laundry service - dorms from $15, singles/doubles from $45.

The Victoria Hotel, 215 Little Collins Street, ph 9653 0441 - good location, large and very popular - from $42.

City Centre Private Hotel, 22 Little Collins Street, ph 9654 5401 - close to transport, clean, basic facilities - from $35.

Serviced Apartments

Riverside Serviced Apartments, 474 Flinders Street, ph 9283 7633 - very hip and spacious apartments, one-to-three-bedroom accommodation, good facilities, long-term stays welcome - from $150.

Oakford Gordon Place, 24 Little Bourke Street, ph 1800 818 236 - good accommodation with lovely atmosphere, pool - from $145.

Holiday Inn Park Suites, 333 Exhibition Street, ph 9663 3333 - standard and roomy accommodation with distinctive decor, sauna, heated rooftop pool - from $140.

Motels

City Limits Motel, 20 Little Bourke Street, ph 9662 2544 - budget prices reflect the basic facilities - from $75.

City Square Motel, 67 Swanston Street, ph 9654 7011 - adequate but nothing out of the ordinary - from $69.

Pubs

Duke of Wellington Hotel, 146 Finders Street, ph 9650 4984 - great location, walking distance to parks and sporting venues, favourite with the city's football supporters, simple and unpretentious accommodation - from $45.

Hostels and Guesthouses

Exford, 199 Russell Street, ph 9663 2697 - good location, clean and very comfortable - dorms from $12, singles/doubles from $39.

Toad Hall, 441 Elizabeth Street, ph 9600 9010 - close to public transport, friendly staff, popular - dorms from $16, singles/doubles from $27.

Backpackers City Inn, 197 Bourke Street, ph 9650 2734 - hardly salubrious setting but cheap breakfasts, includes tour information and booking service - from $14.

North Melbourne

Mid-Range Hotels

Old Melbourne Hotel, 5-17 Flemington Road, ph 9329 9344 - 226 rooms, three restaurants and two bars, nice courtyard, pool - from $146.

Serviced Apartments

City Gardens Apartments, 335 Abbotsford St, ph 9320 6600 - reasonable one to three-bedroom apartments - from $124.

Hostels and Guesthouses

Chapman Gardens YHA, 76 Chapman Street, ph 9328 3595 - small but extremely friendly, outside barbecue, free use of bikes, lovely garden setting - dorms from $15, singles/doubles from $38.

Queensberry Hill YHA, 78 Howard Street, ph 9329 8599 - massive establishment with over 300 rooms, great facilities including a travel agency and *bureau de change*, noticeboard jam-packed with traveller information, good bathrooms, free use of bikes, easy walking distance to Queen Victoria Market and the city centre, excellent value - dorms from $17, singles/doubles from $37.

Global Backpackers Hostel, 238 Victoria Street, ph 9328 3728 - hostel located above the Public Bar Hotel (one of Melbourne's premier venues for live music), sometimes gloomy and unkempt rooms, lively atmosphere, great location - dorms from $11, singles/doubles from $25.

East Melbourne

Upmarket Hotels

Hilton on the Park, 192 Wellington Parade, ph 9419 2000 - ideal location for sporting boffins and nature lovers as the city's major sporting venues and gardens are within easy walking distance, packages available for sporting, theatre and entertainment events, excellent facilities, often host to international touring acts, sauna and spa, pool- from $195.

Boutique Hotels

Magnolia Court Boutique Hotel, 101 Powlett Street, ph 9419 4222 - 25 ensuite rooms, family-run establishment, efficient and very friendly service, good breakfasts, laundry facilities, walking distance to city and sporting venues, excellent value - from $105.

(Overleaf) Olympian sculpture plastered on fashionabe, Nonda Katsilidas-designed city apartment.(above) Head-turning relief adorning one of Melbourne University's many buildings.(below)

(Facing) Melbourne's iconic, freshly painted, Federation-style Flinders Street Station.(above) Busker with bagpipes 'beneath the clocks' of the Flinders Street Station.(below)

Serviced Apartments

Metro Inn Apartment Hotel, 133 Jolimont Road, ph 9654 2844 - 140 one and two-bedroom fully contained apartments, brasserie, gymnasium, pool - from $145.

East Melbourne Apartment Hotel, 25 Hotham Street, ph 9412 2555 - elegant setting, fully equipped kitchenettes, room attendants on call, easy walking distance to gardens, sporting venues and the city centre, price includes breakfast - from $105.

Albert Heights Serviced Apartments, 83 Albert Street, ph 9419 0955 - spacious rooms, reasonable value - from $103.

Eastern Townhouses, 90 Albert Street, ph 9418 6666 - family-run establishment, good alternative to the Albert Heights apartments, stylish setting, pleasant rooftop garden, gym, spa - from $96.

Motels

Treasury Motor Lodge, 179 Powlett Street, ph 9417 5281 - 21 units, basic accommodation - from $90.

George Powlett Lodge, cnr George and Powlett Streets, ph 9419 9488 - 45 units, limited facilities, again only average value - from $80.

B&Bs

Georgian Court Guesthouse, 21 George Street, ph 9419 6353 - cosy single, double and family rooms, good information service, tour bookings, price includes breakfast - from $55.

Pubs

East Melbourne Hotel, 2 Hotham Street, ph 9419 2040 - newly renovated rooms, TV lounge and free off-street parking, excellent food from the downstairs café/bar, easy walking distance to city and the MCG, top value - from $40.

Fitzroy

Serviced Apartments

Royal Gardens Quest Inn, 8 Royal Lane, ph 9419 9888 - one to three-bedroom apartments (some with private court yard/balcony), cradled in large gardens, good facilities, spa, solar-heated pool - from $165.

Hostels and Guesthouses

Nunnery, 116 Nicholson Street, ph 9419 8637 - excellent value, source of travel information, friendly - from $28.

Carlton

Mid-Range Hotels

Carlton Clocktower Quest Inn, 255 Drummond Street, ph 9349 9700 - nestled within the spacious Clocktower shopping and conference complex, large one and two-bedroom apartments, fully equipped kitchen, laundry, free undercover parking, another haunt of interstate business types - from $135.

The Townhouse Carlton, 701 Swanston Street, ph 9347 7811 - close to Melbourne University and Lygon Street shops, also popular with business travellers, sauna and spa - from $125.

Serviced Apartments

Lygon Quest Lodging, 700 Lygon Street, ph 9345 3888 - unremarkable location opposite the city cemetery, clean - from $110.

Motels

Downtowner on Lygon, 66 Lygon Street, ph 9663 5555 - the facade has recently been spruced up giving the place a fresher and more contemporary image, nice courtyard, bar and restaurant, family rooms, close to shopping, eating and entertainment spots, spa - from $119.

Richmond

Mid-Range Hotels

Rydges Riverwalk, 649 Bridge Street, ph 9246 1200 - impressive establishment located on the banks of the Yarra River and overlooking leafy parkland, for many years a Richmond landmark, excellent facilities including large and tidy rooms, two restaurants, a 10-minute tram ride to the city centre, good value - from $150.

Hostels and Guesthouses

Richmond Hill Guesthouse, 353 Church Street, ph 9428 6501 - variety of rooms to choose from, very friendly - dorms from $18, singles/doubles from $35.

Central Accommodation, 21 Bromham Place, ph 9427 8626 - reasonably modern facilities, walking distance to Bridge Road - dorms from $12, singles/doubles from $14.

South Melbourne
Mid-Range Hotels
Parkroyal on St Kilda Rd, 562 St Kilda Road, ph 9529 8888 - stylish accommodation, service could be better-from $190.
Travelodge St Kilda Road, cnr St Kilda Road and Park Street, ph 9209 9888 - good location close to the city centre, gardens and sights, price includes breakfast - from $155.

Port Melbourne
Serviced Apartments
Station Pier Condominiums, 15 Beach Street, ph 9647 9666 - 54 rooms, excellent location right on the beach, one of the city's standouts for accommodation, good rooms and convention facilities, well-tended gardens, jacuzzi, tennis court, gymnasium, sauna, pool - from $220.

Middle Park
Pubs
Middle Park Hotel, 102 Canterbury Road, ph 9690 1958 - great value if you can stomach the vast scrums of yuppies that come carousing here each weekend - from $40.

Albert Park
Pubs
Hotel Victoria, 123 Beaconsfield Parade, ph 9690 3666 - lovely old hotel in good location, great food, large rooms - from $90.

Toorak
Boutique Hotels
Toorak Manor Boutique Hotel, 220 Williams Road, ph 9827 2689 - 12 rooms, small but charming establishment with a cornucopia of Victoriana, very romantic, price includes silver-service breakfast - from $145.

South Yarra
Upmarket Hotels
The Hotel Como, 630 Chapel Street, ph 9824 0400 - much favoured by entertainment types, mixture of studio and

suite accommodation (some with spa baths), close to the areas best shops and restaurants, high level of security and privacy, fantastic food, gymnasium, spa and sauna, pool - from $460 (weekend packages drastically reduce prices to a more affordable $270).

Boutique Hotels

Tilba Hotel, 30 Toorak Road, ph 9867 8844 - exquisite and very appealing olde worlde accommodation - from $125.

Serviced Apartments

South Yarra Hill Suites, 14 Murphy Street, ph 9868 8222 - cosy and stylish accommodation, spa and sauna, pool - from $199.

Manor House Apartments, 23 Avoca Street, ph 9867 1266 - fully equipped rooms, good location close to Toorak Road and Chapel Street - from $75.

Hostels and Guesthouses

Lords Lodge Backpackers, 204 Punt Rd, ph 9510 5658 - ramshackle but cosy accommodation, tourist information, bike hire, personal lockers, free tea and coffee, clean and basic - dorms from $13, singles/doubles from $14.

St Kilda

Upmarket Hotels

Novotel Bayside Melbourne, 16 The Esplanade, ph 9525 5522 - lovely position opposite the bay (the top storeys, naturally, have fantastic views), easy walking distance to both Acland and Fitzroy Streets, rather characterless but has loads of facilities including free undercover parking, spa and sauna, hot tub, gymnasium, heated pool - from $140.

Serviced Apartments

Barkly Quest Lodge, 170-80 Barkly Street, ph 9525 5000 - 26 fully equipped apartments, simple but clean - from $105.

Redan Quest Lodging, 25 Redan Street, ph 9529 7595 - fully equipped apartments, laidback atmosphere, leafy location close to Chapel Street - from $75.

B&Bs

Robinsons by the Sea, 335 Beaconsfield Parade, ph 9534 2683 - small but lovely setting in a refurbished terrace house, book one of the balcony rooms - from $130.

Victoria House B&B, 57 Mary Street, ph 9525 4512 - another lovely setting, courtyard, great value - from $75.

Motels

Crest International Motel, 47 Barkly Street, ph 9537 1788 - 1970s decor a feature, conference facilities, restaurant, good value - from $89.

Charnwood Motor Inn, 3 Charnwood Road, ph 9525 4199 - quiet location - from $55.

Hostels and Guesthouses

Olembia Guesthouse, 96 Barkly Street, ph 9537 1412 - grand accommodation in a beautifully restored Edwardian house, very laidback atmosphere, courtyard, laundry and kitchen facilities, good clean rooms, free tea and coffee, very popular - dorms from $15, singles/doubles from $35.

Enfield House Backpackers, 2 Enfield Street, ph 9534 8159 - massive and rambling establishment, budget traveller favourite, friendly and very informative staff, great noticeboard, traveller pick-up service - dorms from $16, singles/doubles from $25.

Ritz Backpackers, 169 Fitzroy Street, ph 9525 3501 - haunt of British budget travellers, free tea and coffee, good facilities including women-only dorms, can get noisy at night, clean - dorms from $14, singles/doubles from $34.

St Kilda Coffee Palace Backpackers Inn, 24 Grey Street, ph 9534 5283 - close to all the area's best cafés and restaurants, St Kilda landmark, huge establishment with over 100 rooms, 16 bathrooms, two laundries, pool room, rooftop garden (great views) and barbecue, noticeboard an excellent source of traveller information, spacious kitchen, friendly staff, lots of activities including pub crawls, popular video evenings, great value - dorms from $11, singles/doubles from $28.

Kookaburra Cottage, 56 Jackson Street, ph 9534 5457 - small and friendly, bike hire, can arrange a number of organised tours, tiny rooms, free tea and coffee - dorms from $12, singles/doubles from $14.

Leopard House, cnr Grey and Jackson Streets, ph 9534 1200 - attractive and airy setting, weekly barbecue, bike hire, comfortable TV lounge, outside courtyard, free pick-up, good value - dorms from $12.

Getting Around

Melbourne's growth since its founding has been dizzying. The city centre and outlying suburbs now cover over 6000 sq km, making it one of the largest metropolitan regions in the world. Thankfully getting around such a large area is made relatively easy by major forms of public transport such as trains, buses, taxis and the city's distinctive, ramblingly functional trams.

Public Transport

The Met is Melbourne's public transport system. It operates trains, buses and trams which usually run Monday to Saturday between 5am and midnight, and Sunday from 8am to 11pm. Tickets can be purchased on board trams and buses, at train stations and from selected vending and validating machines (city-wide automatic ticketing will be available in late 1997), or from the City Met Shop, 103 Elizabeth Street. Newsagents and some takeaway shops and milk bars also sell tickets. Note that tickets can't be purchased in bulk. Also remember that being caught without a ticket on any of the services can mean a $100 on-the-spot fine.

Three fare zones apply in the metropolitan area. The type of ticket you buy (either paper or scratch and colour coded by zone) depends on which zone you intend travelling in and for how long. Zone 1 tickets cover the city centre and inner city/suburban areas, while Zones 2 and 3 radiate to Melbournes outer limits. Two hour, daily, weekly, monthly and yearly tickets provide unlimited travel and are, in the main, remarkably cheap.

There are also 60 Plus tickets (a daily ticket for people 60 years and over who are Victorian residents), Zone 1 Short Trip tickets (giving 10 rides for the price of eight in Zone 1), Off-Peak Saver tickets (weekday discount travel to the city from Zones 2 and 3) plus a host of other special deals. Further information is available from the Met

Information Centre, ph 13 1638, the friendly and very informative City Met Shop, and train stations.

Domestic and international visitors should make the most of Melbourne's excellent public transport system; in early 1997 the state government announced its privatisation by the end of 1998.

Trains

Melbourne's train network is generally good and reaches most parts of the metropolitan area. Trains tend to be much faster than buses or trams and usually run every seven minutes during peak hour, and every 20 minutes during non-peak hours. On some routes such as the Sandringham line trains run every 10 minutes regardless of the hour.

According to the Public Transport Corporation (PTC) an 'on-time' train is one arriving within five minutes of its scheduled time (meaning any train arriving five minutes late is technically on time). Unfortunately, late-arriving trains are becoming more frequent due to equipment failure, suicides (an increasing Melbourne phenomenon) and worker malaise brought on by pending privatisation. Video monitors display arrival and departure times in the city centre stations while similar information is available at suburban stations via touch-type recorder boxes.

The city's main terminals are the historic and mustard-coloured Flinders Street Station, and the modernistic and colourless Spencer Street Station. The latter is where country Victoria and interstate services leave from.

Buses

The citys buses are mostly used for short-distance travel to areas without train lines (Fitzroy, Carlton, South Melbourne and Port Melbourne). The fleet is slowly being updated, and services run every 20 minutes.

If you're stranded in the city after midnight you can catch a NightRider Bus. This service departs from the City Square hourly between 12.30-4.30am on weekends, with routes covering most of the metropolitan area.

For interstate bus services contact Greyhound Pioneer, ph 13 2030, and McCaffertys, ph 9670 2533.

Trams

Melbournes first trams, which were horse-drawn, arrived in 1884. Five years later the first electric tram was introduced. Today there are 630 trams operating on 28 routes, with lines extending over 220km.

Trams have retained their nostalgic appeal (who can mistake the rattle of wheels and the tintinnabulation of bells) and continue to provide an efficient means of getting around and seeing the city. In recent years some trams have been splashily decorated by national artists including Michael Leunig and Reg Mombassa, used as restaurants (see the Eating Out chapter), venues for theatre, or hired out for private functions. Their only real drawback is that they are sometimes subject to the vagaries of traffic, eg vehicles blocking tracks, conductors helping passengers with prams and/or heavy loads on and off. Delays can also be caused when trams are staffed by drivers only, leading to long queues as money is exchanged and tickets clipped. To compensate, allow plenty of time if journeying from one side of the city to the other during peak-hour traffic.

The City Circle Tram, a refurbished W-class tram painted in distinctive burgundy and cream, travels a city circuit (including Flinders, Spring, Nicholson, La Trobe and Spencer Streets) and passes many of the citys premier tourist attractions along the way. Conductors (or Customer Service Employees as they're officially called) are a good source of information, while an electronic commentary offers banal comments on various sights to bemused tourists and sandwich-munching office workers.

The service is free, and can be caught at a number of specially marked stops in the city centre. It runs daily every 10 minutes from 10am-6pm, and takes about 30 minutes. It also has links with other transport routes.

Taxi

There are over 3200 taxis in the metropolitan area, though sometimes (especially late at night) they seem surprisingly thin on the ground. Taxis can be hired on the street, at designated ranks (Bourke and Lonsdale Streets), Flinders and Spencer Street stations, major hotels or by

phoning the following companies:
Arrow Taxi Services, ph 9417 1111
Black Cabs Combined, ph 13 2227
Embassy Taxis, ph 13 1755
Melbourne Combined, ph 13 1323
Silver Top Taxi Service, ph 131 008
West Suburban, ph 9689 1144.

Selected taxis are also equipped to take passengers in wheel chairs, while others can be ordered with child seats and infant capsules. And mirroring New York, all new taxis are now required to be yellow in colour.

Car

Melburnians are notoriously intemperate drivers. According to a recent poll conducted by *The Age*, the city's car owners not only believe they own the road, they're also prepared to flout a range of traffic regulations to reduce travel times. As a rule of thumb, don't be timid or overly respectful once on the road as this technique will often confuse the natives.

To add to the general chaos, some of Melbourne's road rules are among the most quixotic in the country. The 'hook turn' is a prime example. At some intersections in the city centre, cars turning right must queue in the left-hand lane, then wait (even if the coast is clear) until the light turns from green to orange. Only then is it possible to make a right-hand turn. Other risky aspects of car travel include trams (which are dangerously large, can only be overtaken on the left, or not at all when stopping to pick up or put down passengers), the state of the city's roads (a mess of potholes, ridges, bumps and tram tracks), and general congestion.

The speed limit in built-up areas is a comfortable 60km/h and between 100-110 km/h on highways (speed cameras are common and frequently rotated). Seat-belts must be worn at all times. Penalties for drink driving - the blood alcohol limit is .05 - are strictly enforced.

Car Rental

Cars can be hired from the following agencies:
Astoria, ph 9347 7766
Avis, ph 9663 6366

Budget, ph 13 2727
Crown, ph 9662 2011
Delta, ph 13 1390
Dollar, ph 9326 9999
Hertz, ph 13 30 39
Thrifty, ph 9663 5200

Remember care hire will often earn frequent flyer points.

Parking

Even though the city centre has over 10,000 meters and 40,000 off-street car spaces, parking can still be a problem. Meters variously take 10c, 20c, $1 and $2 coins while hourly rates for carparks (just follow the arrow signs for their location) vary between $2-6. Some carparks also offer discounts to moviegoers and shoppers (eg Melbourne Central). If you can't find a car space bear in mind that the city council collects more than $3 million annually in weekend fines and meter payments, and can fine drivers up to $50 at an expired meter.

A handy little guide to pick up is *City Access Car Parking.* It includes location maps and listings of all the citys carparks, advice on where you can park for $2 an hour, overnight parking spots, and supportive tips on making your visit to the city as hassle-free as possible. Copies are available from the City Council, ph 9658 9800.

Bicycle

Melbourne is an eminently cyclable destination, due largely to its flat terrain, often spectacular scenery and an extensive network of good quality tracks. Some of the city's most popular bike routes are along Royal Parade and Sydney and St Kilda Roads. Longer routes include:

Yarra Path - follows the scenic Yarra River and runs from Princes Bridge in the city to Westerfold Park, Templestowe.

Princes Park Drive - runs between Princes Park, around the expansive Melbourne General Cemetery to Melbourne University and the city.

Footscray Road - runs from the Maribyrnong River down Footscray Road and links up with the Yarra River.

Bicycle Rental

Bikes can be hired from the following shops:

Borsari Cycles, 193 Lygon Street, Carlton, ph 9347 4100
Mascot Cycles, 308 Bridge Road, Richmond, ph 9428 4122
St Kilda Cycles, 11 Carlisle Street, St Kilda, ph 9534 3074

Ferry

One of Melbourne's most popular ferry operators is *Williamstown Bay and River Cruises*, 15 Thompson Street, Williamstown, ph 9397 2255. The company has two ferries - MV *John Batman* and MV *Victoria* - which ply between the World Trade Centre, Southgate and St Kilda Pier to Gem Pier in Williamstown. Timetable information is available by calling 9596 4144.

Transport to/from the Airport

For information about Melbourne's Tullamarine International Airport see the Travel Tips chapter.

From the airport, Skybuses depart every 30 minutes from 5.40am-11.30pm (timetables available from in front of the Domestic Arrivals area) to the city centre and Spencer Street Station. Tickets, which cost $9 for adults and $4.50 for children, can be bought from the coach driver or the Travellers Information Service on the ground floor of the International Terminal.

From the city centre, Skybuses depart from Spencer Street Station and the Melbourne Transit Centre, 58 Franklin St. Courtesy bus connections to/from city hotels, Spencer Street Station and other stops can be arranged.

If money is no obstacle, Airport Transfer Service, ph 9879 0144, provide chauffeur-driven luxury cars and stretch limousines between the airport and city. A similar service for up to seven passengers (with child seats and infant capsules) is also offered by AC Chauffeur Drive, ph 13 2121.

A taxi between the airport and city centre costs around $25-30 depending on the traffic conditions.

Eating Out

The subject of food is the source of endless discussion among Melburnians (after staying at home, eating out is their favourite pastime). Consider just some of the city's epicurean delights - sourdough baguettes, Richard Thomas cheeses, Alligator-brand pastas, well-built crustaceans, sharp-tasting fruit tarts, and Ricketts Point ice-cream - and you begin to appreciate their culinary zeal. Obviously, Melburnians cannot live by rocket and parmesan alone.

Melbourne has always considered itself the culinary capital of Australia (Sydney would vehemently disagree, believing it has now stolen a march on its southern neighbour). Once gold petered out the city's burgeoning ethnic population turned to growing lush market gardens and importing foodstuffs from their homeland. Their skills and endeavours have since brought spice and colour to many dishes, and lifted the food from the profanely mundane to the often ridiculously sublime.

Increasingly, eating out in Melbourne is a tale of excellent meals and good eateries. In the past five years the city has rediscovered quality, service and credible prices - prerequisites for a dynamic and evolving cuisine. You can dine in sidewalk cafés or in one of Melbourne's flagship restaurants, and pay as little as $4 for a meal or as much as $200. Most are either licensed (which means the establishment can sell alcohol on the premises) or Bring Your Own (BYO), meaning patrons can bring their own alcohol with them.

For all the good oil on wining and dining in Melbourne (for both budget and cashed-up travellers) pick up a copy of *The Age Good Food Guide 1997*. Its available at bookshops and major newsagents for $16.95.

In addition, Melbourne has a diverse range of food tours (see the Tours chapter for further information).

City Centre
Chinese

Ong International Food Court, 265 Little Bourke Street, ph 9662 3416 - oodles of stalls selling everything from short soups to zesty curries, very cheap.

Shark Fin House, 131 Little Bourke Street, ph 9663 1555 - Asian mainstay, popular with business types, superb yum cha and Peking Duck.

Shark Fin Inn, 50 Little Bourke Street, ph 9662 2681 - original trendsetter, modern facilities combined with traditional food, includes courtyard.

Mask of China, 115-117 Little Bourke Street, ph 9662 2116 - a Szechuan region and modern Asian specialist, boasts great game and seafood dishes plus good wines and service from a bevy of Suzie Wong lookalikes (sadly, no one remotely resembled William Holden while I was there).

Empress of China, 120 Little Bourke Street, ph 9663 1883 - over 25 years in business, small and very popular with corporate bigwigs.

Fortuna Village, 235 Little Bourke Street, ph 9663 3044 - northern regional cuisine, Peking-style yum cha, seafood and lots of it.

Kun Ming Café, 212 Little Bourke Street, ph 9663 1851 - cheap and basic, service can be slow but worth the wait.

Fortuna Village, 235 Little Bourke Street, ph 9663 3044 - near the top of the heap when it comes to the city's best Chinese restaurants, interesting food at good prices.

Bamboo House, 47 Little Bourke Street, ph 9662 1565 - award-winner and haunt of local politicians - regional and Peking-style dishes, quite expensive.

Flower Drum, 17 Market Lane, ph 9662 3655 - peerless food (the Peking Duck is to die for) in an enormous space that possesses a *feng shui* rightness to it, another great favourite with political heavyweights and the city's movers and shakers - private and function rooms, unforgettable service, very expensive.

Supper Inn, 15-17 Celestial Ave, ph 9663 4759 - some of the choicest and least expensive Cantonese food in the city.

Dragon Boat Restaurant, Central Hotel, cnr Flinders and

Spencer Streets, ph 9629 8388 - yum cha specialists.

King of Kings, 209 Russell Street, ph 9663 2895 - fast, cheap eating at formica tables.

Silks, Crown Casino complex, ph 9292 6888 - Cantonese dishes in lustrous surroundings, very expensive so make sure you dine before playing the tables.

Thai

Sawasdee, 139 Little Bourke Street, ph 9663 4052 - consistent award winner for authentic Thai food.

Italian

Pellegrini's, 66 Bourke Street, ph 9662 1885 - Melbourne landmark ever since it opened in 1954, distinctive European atmosphere, home of the city's best coffee, sweeping bar always filled to overflowing with actors, artists, business people, politicians and students - cheap and humongous servings of pasta and lasagne, great pastries and toasted sandwiches, don't miss it!

Florentino, No 80 Bourke Street, ph 9662 1811 - very urbane setting, renowned for its Caesar salads, irrepressible service provided by a small army of waiters, excellent business lunches.

Florentine Cellar Bar, 80 Bourke Street, ph 9662 1811 - downstairs in the Florentino, another city institution, popular meeting place for the young and moneyed, cheap pasta and minestrone dishes, stylish.

Caffe Cento Venti, 120 Collins Street, ph 9650 5621 - one for the smart set, tenderly dressed food that includes good risotto and chicken dishes, wide ranging wine list, very popular, quite pricey so don't come to graze.

Café Bove, 439 Little Collins Street, ph 9606 0130 - good strong coffee supported by a range of tasty snacks.

Il Bacaro, 168 Little Collins Street, ph 9654 6778 - voted best new restaurant by *The Age Good Food Guide* - innovative design and food that is Melbourne's current trendsetter, café atmosphere, small and simple menu featuring pasta, fish, salads and vegetables, great cocktails and wine to aid digestion and stimulate conversation.

Caffe Nardini, 510 Elizabeth Street, ph 9663 1910 - wonderfully inviting ambience, inside and outside dining, good food, formerly known as *Le Marche*.

L'Incontro Café, Swanston Street, ph 9650 9603 - modern

café with Italian pretensions, raised above footpath to provide more glamour and better views through the glass walls - mixed food and service.

Marchettis Latin Restaurant, 55 Lonsdale Street, ph 9662 1985 - Melbourne institution that serves good but not challenging food, great service, small but comfortable bar, fabulous wines and cocktails, very cosmopolitan, popular for both lunches or dinners - expensive.

Waiters Restaurant, 20 Meyer's Place, ph 9650 1508 - great service and good plain food at cheap prices.

Cecconi's, Crown Casino complex, ph 9292 6887 - humongous establishment featuring mid-range dishes (pasta, antipasti, etc).

International and Contemporary

Walters Wine Bar, Level 3, Southgate, ph 9690 9211 - meeting place for the city's publishers, editors and lesser panjandrums - good food complemented by marvellous wines, excellent views - quite expensive, open late.

Blue Train Café, Level 3, Southgate, ph 9696 0111 - wannabee crowd plus basic food makes this place very popular, arrive early if you want to get a good seat.

Blakes, Ground Level, Southgate, ph 9699 4100 - delicious food from one of Melbourne's celebrity chefs (the city's equivalent to Sydneys Neil Perry of *Rockpool* fame), good wine list, reasonably priced.

Hard Rock Café, 1 Bourke Street, ph 9650 4755 - recently opened establishment that affects celebrity myopia, all burgers, fries, and gushy service, merchandise counter sells T-shirts and assorted paraphernalia, open late.

Café Le Monde, 18 Bourke Street, ph 9663 7804 - lots of pony-tailed men loaded on coffee and gossip, good breakfast, great pastries.

The Nudel Bar, 76 Bourke Street, ph 9662 9100 - specialising in global food-on-the-run (spicy Asian dishes, pasta, lasagne, etc), great value.

Lounge, 243 Swanston Street, ph 9663 2916 - super-cool hangout for the city's bright young things and grunge crowd - verandah seating, large salad bar, pool tables and live entertainment, inexpensive but excellent value.

(Facing) Lygon Street, Melbourne's centre of Italian culture and cuisine.

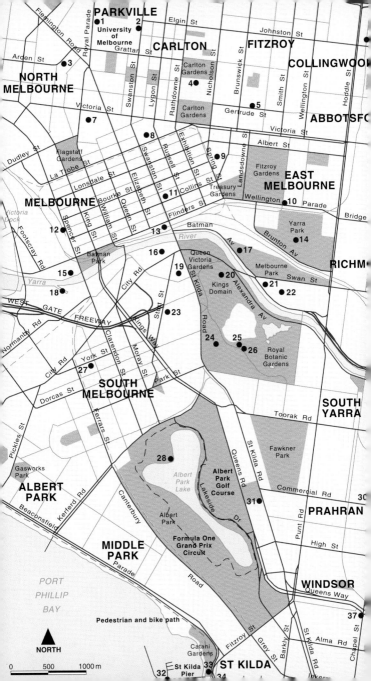

MAP KEY
MELBOURNE CITY AND
SURROUNDING SUBURBS MAP

Accomodation
10. Hilton on the Park
31. Parkroyal on St Kilda Road

Eating
32. Kiosk

Other
1. Percy Grainger Museum
2. Ian Potter Gallery
3. Meat Market Craft Centre
4. Royal Exhibition Centre
5. 200 Gertrude Street Gallery
6. Victoria Park
7. Queen Street Market
8. RMIT
9. Parliament House
11. Melbourne Town Hall
12. Spencer Street Station
13. Flinders Street Station
14. MCG
15. Crown Casino
16. Southgate
17. National Tennis Centre
18. Polly Woodside Maritime Museum
19. Victorian Arts Centre

20. Sidney Myer Music Bowl
21. Sports and Entertainment Centre
22. Olympic Park
23. Malthouse Theatre
24. Shrine of Remembrance
25. La Trobes Cottage
26. Herbarium
27. South Melbourne Market
28. Jolly Roger School of Sailing and Boat Hire
29. Jam Factory
30. Prahran Market
33. Royal Melbourne Yacht Squadron
34. Esplanade Art and Craft Market
35. Luna Park
36. Palais Theatre
37. Astor Theatre

Ecco, 11-25 Crossley Street, ph 9663 3000 - just opened, dimly lit and very noisy, simple menu that includes efficiently executed food (calamari, rissotto, steak), good but not great.

Café Y, The Hotel Y, 489 Elizabeth Street, ph 9329 5188 - cheap muffins and salad rolls, good coffee, quick service, fully licensed, what more could you want?

Bistro 1, 126 Little Collins Street, ph 9654 3343 - European leanings, interesting decor including wooden reliefs of wildlife, some of the best coffee in the city, snacks.

Planet Hollywood/Official All Star Café, Crown Casino complex, ph 9682 7827/9699 8326 - loud music, loud fittings, loud people - avoid if you can.

Japanese

Kenzan, Collins Place, 45 Collins Street, ph 9654 8933 - swish interior with an excellent sushi bar.

Teppanyaki Inn, 182 Collins Street, ph 9650 9431 - top-quality beef and seafood dishes, sushi bar.

Daimaru Sushi Bar, Level 1, Melbourne Central, ph 9660 6666 - one of the best places for Japanese food in the city, extensive and cheap menu, good range of Japanese beers.

Edoya, 138 Russell Street, ph 9654 7358 - delicate food, open every day, not too pricey.

French

Le Restaurant, Hotel Sofitel, 25 Collins Street, ph 9653 0000 - delicate food, magnificent views.

Paul Bocuse, Level 4, Daimaru, 211 La Trobe Street, ph 9660 6600 - superior food courtesy of chef Philippe Mouchel, exquisite service - undoubtedly one of the best restaurants in the country despite its peculiar shopping centre location.

Simply French, 2 City Road, Southgate, ph 9699 9804 - popular hangout for artists, writers, directors and the like - flexible menu, average prices.

Greek

Stalactites, 177 Lonsdale Street, ph 9663 3316 - kitsch decor, okay food, open late.

Tsindos The Greeks Restaurant, 197 Lonsdale Street, ph 9663 3194 - huge meals, live entertainment on weekends, inexpensive.

North Melbourne

Vietnamese

Vietnam House, 284 Victoria Street, ph 9329 7318 - cheap and tasty food.

Dalat Restaurant, 270 Victoria Street, ph 9329 0329 - more of the same.

Italian

A Roma, 408 Queen Street, ph 9606 0530 - located on the ground floor of the fashionable Nonda Katsilidas building across the road from the Queen Victoria Market - haunt of the city's architects, spacious interior that is all dark wood and stainless steel - pizza, panini, pastries and biscuits on display in glass counter, individual daily menus featuring veal shanks and osso bucco ($14), pastas (around $9), *a la mode* Alessi sugar shakers on each table.

Amiconi, 359 Victoria Street, ph 9328 3710 - popular establishment serving old-fashioned Italian fare.

West Melbourne
Pub Grub
Three Crowns Hotel, 365 Victoria Street, ph 9328 4305 - small but cosy bar, fat juicy sausages and mash, big helpings of fish and chips.

Abbotsford
Pub Grub
The Retreat, 226 Nicholson Street, ph 9419 1459 - TV aficionados will remember this pub as the place where the popular Australian TV series *The Sullivans* was filmed - basic but good food including burgers and fish and chips, serves a good selection of draught beer.

Fitzroy
Thai
Sala Thai, 266 Brunswick Street, ph 9417 4929 - well-prepared food, attentive service, cosy setting.
Indian
Sandos Indian Restaurant, 272 Brunswick Street, ph 9419 8472 - fantastic and affordable food.
Chishtis Indian Restaurant, 15 Johnston St, ph 9417 6237 - excellent alternative to Sandos, friendly service, cheap.
Italian
Marios, 303 Brunswick Street, ph 9417 3343 - the strips standout for service and good food, consistently judged as the place to go for the city's best coffee - won't break your budget.
International and Contemporary
Café Provincial, cnr Brunswick and Johnston Streets, ph 9417 2228 - trendy eatery in great location, minimalist decor - delicious food including wood-fired pizzas with toppings such as spiced lamb, pesto and goat cheese, and smoked salmon and spring onion - very affordable.
The Fitz Café, 347 Brunswick Street, ph 9417 5794 - big on breakfasts (bacon and eggs smothered in hollandaise sauce plus pancakes, muesli, etc), try the popular Fitz

Brekkie Special for $8, outside tables - food can get ordinary once staff are busy.

Rhumbarellas, 342 Brunswick St, ph 9417 5652 - size of an aeroplane hangar, good antipasto and soup, okay value.

Babka, 358 Brunswick Street, ph 9416 0091 - renowned for its breads (yummy casalinga) and pastries, great breakfasts, good service, popular on Sunday morning.

Bistro Inferno, 302 Brunswick Street, ph 9416 0953 - sparkling fresh and spicy food, cheap.

Black Cat Café, 252 Johnston Street, ph 9419 2206 - inner-city favourite, raffish interior, large menu with lots of interesting items, excellent prices.

The Artists Café, 350 Nicholson Street, ph 9417 4922 - recently renovated, interior dominated by three enormous paintings by Charles Billich, bohemian atmosphere - menu comprising standard dishes (oysters, antipasto, carpaccio) plus more interesting variations (veal chops on saffron risotto), uninspiring mash, service could be better.

Japanese

Akari, 177 Brunswick Street, ph 9419 3786 - tasty food served on handmade ceramics, wide selection of Japanese beers, early dinner specials.

Spanish

De Los Santos, 175 Brunswick Street, ph 9417 1567 - lively little place, often good music, cheap tapas.

Carmen Bar, 74 Johnston Street, ph 9417 4794 - no-thrills food, live entertainment most weekends.

Pub Grub

Standard Hotel, 293 Fitzroy Street, Fitzroy, ph 9419 4793 - popular local hangout, surprisingly diverse menu that has everything from burgers to osso bucco with risotto, great range of beers.

Cyber Cafés

Online Café at the Melting Pot Café, 357 Smith Street, ph 9419 5789 - range of multimedia experiences, training courses in surfing the Internet starting from $50 for three hours, good coffee and snacks.

Carlton

Malaysian

Chinta Ria, 118-20 Elgin Street, ph 9349 2599 - fine cuisine including coconut and chilli-infused laksas, intimate atmosphere, good R&B music.

Casa Malaya, 118 Lygon Street, ph 9663 7068 - good, affordable food in pleasant surroundings.

Thai

Lemongrass, 189 Lygon Street, ph 9347 5204 - one of the city's better Thai restaurants, good menu and service, excellent smorgasbord lunches, quite pricey.

Poppy's Thai Restaurant, 230 Lygon St, ph 9663 3366 - every thing from Thai fish cakes to green coconut curry chicken.

Italian

Tiamo, 303 Lygon Street, ph 9347 5759 - the name means 'I love you' in Italian, family-run establishment that has been operating for 20 years, quite small and dimly lit with wooden tables and benches, old-fashioned homely Italian cooking, very friendly atmosphere and service, cheap pastas, good desserts, great value.

Tiamo 2, 305 Lygon Street, 9347 0911 - run by the same family and right next door, more wooden tables, benches and comfort food, similar menu to Tiamo including focaccia, antipasto, char-grilled vegetables, and polpettone (meat loaf) - blackboard lists dishes of the day, very popular with Carlton regulars.

Borsari, 201 Lygon Street, ph 9349 1444 - good-value meals at inexpensive prices.

Da Salvatore Restaurant, 132 Lygon Street, ph 9663 4778 - choice of round and rectangular pizzas, good topping, crisp salads, hangout for local celebrities.

Universita Bar and Ristorante, 255 Lygon Street, ph 9347 2142 - Lygon Street staple since 1952, great espresso coffee, simple but hearty cuisine with fantastic soups and pastas - popular with families and students, very cheap.

La Porchetta, 392 Rathdowne Street, ph 9347 8906 - cheap pasta and pizza, huge salads, good service considering how maniacally busy they get.

Papa Ginos, 221 Lygon Street, ph 9347 5758 - slightly more expensive pasta/pizza than La Porchetta but just as tasty.

International and Contemporary

Jimmy Watson's, 333 Lygon Street, ph 9347 3985 - popular watering hole and restaurant for academics, students and former radicals, traditional food served with verve and style, great selection of wines, reasonably priced.

Trotters, 400 Lygon Street, ph 9347 5657 - great breakfast menus, good pasta.

Wine Bar II, 166 Rathdowne Street, ph 9349 4999 - swish bar with above-average food.

Toofeys, 162 Elgin Street, ph 9347 9838 - the best fish restaurant in the city, comfortable environment, speedy service, haunt of local and city workers, academics, politicians and showbiz types - extremely fast service.

Richmond

Malaysian

Chilli Padi, 18 Bridge Road, ph 9428 6432 - traditional Malaysian tucker with good laksa and noodle dishes (try the mee goreng) - lovely environment, friendly staff, budget prices.

Vietnamese

Tho Tho, 66 Victoria Street, ph 9428 5833 - a real standout, modern setting, scrumptious food including crispy quail and mouth-watering rice paper rolls - good wine and beer list, very cheap, great value.

Vao Doi, 120 Victoria Street, ph 9428 3264 - cheap and tasty, very friendly.

Que Huong, 176 Bridge Rd,ph 9429 5900-more of the same.

Thai

Thy Thy 1, 142 Victoria Street, ph 9429 1104 - Richmond favourite, consistently good food and absurdly low prices, can get busy.

Thai Oriental Café and Takeaway, 430 Bridge Road, ph 9428 4271 - curries, noodles and pappadums galore.

International and Contemporary

The Tofu Shop, 78 Bridge Road, ph 9429 6204 - popular hangout for the healthy minded, large salads, rolls, spinach pastries and pies.

Vlados Charcoal Grill, 61 Bridge Road, ph 428 5833 - great servings of porterhouse steak (from only the best ox beef) and other meats cooked over coals - vegetarians and the squeamish have been known to leave the premises convulsing - quite pricey.

Greek

Elatos Greek Tavern, 213 Swan Street, ph 9428 5683 - good, reasonably priced food and a great atmosphere, perfect place for a party booking.

Agapi, 262 Swan Street, ph 9428 8337 - more authentic Greek food, affordable.

Pub Grub

All Nations Hotel, 64 Lennox Street, ph 9428 5612 - glorious open-fire setting, great meat-loaf and beef pies (around $10), lashings of mashed potatoes and sauerkraut, excellent range of beers.

Cyber Cafés

Cyber Café Australia, 541 Church Street, ph 9429 1311 - specialty cakes, focaccias, home-made soups and rolls, rather uninspired coffee, friendly and attentive staff - 20 cents per minute, $6 per half-hour Internet connection.

Kew

Studley Park Boathouse Café, Boathouse Road, ph 9853 1828 - historic weatherboard building in a riverside setting of umbrella-dotted lawns, eucalyptus and elms - eclectic yuppie-style food (duck rillettes, herb-crusted chicken breast, seafood mousse ravioli), small wine list, pricey.

Hawthorn

Chinese

Panda Restaurant, 815 Glenferrie Road, ph 9819 4795 - Cantonese food and hospitality to the max, popular.

Malaysian

Penang Coffee House, 359 Burwood Road, ph 9819 2092 - unquestionably the best laksa, mee goreng and black sticky rice pudding in Melbourne, very affordable.

International and Contemporary

Stephanie's, 405 Tooronga Road, ph 9822 8944 - Hawthorn flagship restaurant located in a charming old house (check out the fairy lights on the trees outside), run by chef and author Stephanie Alexander, enormous space with six dining rooms and two kitchens, impressionist-style food that is both ambitious and eminently edible, expensive but perfect for those special occasions.

South Yarra

Thai

Thai 505, 505 Chapel Sreett, ph 9827 8682 - excellent food, seating limited.

Chiangmai Thai Restaurant, 427 Chapel Street, ph 9826 1181 - good value and service.

Italian

Pieroni, 172 Toorak Road, ph 9827 7833 - stylish setting, extensive food and wine list.

Barolo, 74 Toorak Road, ph 9866 2744 - affordable Italian fare in nice setting.

Caffe e Cucina, 581 Chapel Street, ph 9827 4139 - quintessential and fashionable Melbourne eatery, small seating (just under 50) means patrons are often spilling onto the street, great food and wine, superb service, a must.

International and Contemporary

Carmines, 62 Toorak Road, ph 9820 0238 - quick and interesting food, flexible menu.

Chinois, 176 Toorak Road, ph 9826 3388 - Chinese meets West cuisine, good service, French Sunday brunch with jazz.

Harveys Restaurant, 10 Murphy Street, ph 9867 3605 - great breakfasts including muesli and Eggs Benedict, popular with local celebrities.

Tonic, 564 Chapel Street, ph 9826 5011 - preposterously groovy bar-cum-restaurant, serves reasonable food, distracted and often disinterested service.

Maxims, 632 Chapel Street, ph 9866 5500 - elegant environment, good dependable menu, very popular so bookings essential, quite pricey.

Japanese

Kanpai, 569 Chapel Street, ph 9827 4379 - express service, huge and informative menu, unpretentious food, great desserts (try the delicious red bean cake), very affordable.

French

The South Yarra Café, 177 Toorak Road, ph 9827 2648 - smallish, white linen table-cloths with Impressionist prints on the walls, southern French cuisine, limited and quite expensive wine list, okay value.

France-Soir, 11 Toorak Road, ph 9866 8569 - Melbourne's

first and still best authentic Parisian bistro, stylish setting, great wine list, simple but filling food, pricey.

Prahran

Malaysian

Chinta Ria, 176 Commercial Road, ph 9510 6520 - consistently good food from the Chinta chain run by Simon Goh, nice jazzy sounds, nice prices.

Vietnamese

Saigon Rose, 206 Chapel Street, ph 9510 9651 - cheap and wholesome food, good vegetarian meals.

Thai

Patee Thai, 135 Chapel Street, ph 9510 6618 - one of the city's best Thai joints, big choice of menu items.

Indian

The Jewel of India Restaurant, 373 Chapel Street, ph 9824 1822 - award-winner with exotic and affordable dishes, regional specialties, very popular.

International and Contemporary

Globe Café, 218 Chapel Street, ph 9510 8693 - global cuisine with a decidedly Asian bent, great range of snacks.

Greville Bar, 143 Greville Street, ph 9529 4800 - simple and striking food (deep-fried artichoke is a must), constantly evolving menu, relaxed atmosphere.

Continental Café, 132 Greville Street, ph 9510 2788 - great food and great prices in one of the city's premier establishments, sophisticated and very cool.

Feedwell Café, 97 Greville Street, ph 9510 3128 - organic and macrobiotic foods including burgers, sandwiches, salads and cakes, try the soy lattes and range of juices.

French

Jacques Reymond, 78 Williams Road, ph 9525 2178 - one of Melbourne's most renowned restaurants, awarded 'four hats' in *The Age Good Food Guide*, excellent cuisine with flavours so alive they reach from the plate and grab you by the goolies, expensive.

South Melbourne

Thai

Isthmus of Kra, 50 Park Street, ph 9690 3688 - huge space

with arctic air-conditioning, superb and beautifully presented food (its signature dish is Monsoon oysters baked in a clay dish with lime, chilli and basil), very busy, should not be missed, affordable prices.

Japanese

Kobe, 179 Clarendon Street, ph 6990 2692 - no-frills food matched by economical prices.

St Kilda and Bayside

Malaysian

Chinta Blues, 6 Acland Street, ph 9534 9233 - recently opened hawker bar/café that's become another trendy new addition to St Kilda, cubby-hole location behind the Prince of Wales Hotel, walls adorned by Asian photographs, laidback and always full, cheap and spicy dishes including curry puffs, spring rolls ($3), filling soups ($4), Indian-style *mee goreng* ($7.50), *gado gado* ($7.50) plus brightly coloured desserts, also does good breakfasts of coffee, croissants and *congee*, has takeaways.

Chinta Ria, 94 Acland Street, ph 9525 4664 - excellent food and service, soul-tinged music to the fore.

Vietnamese

Tien Tien Café, 217 Barkly Street, ph 9593 9988 - snazzy interior, reasonable food including good prawn soups, attentive service.

Thai

Coriander Thai, 29 Fitzroy Street, ph 9537 0888 - cheap, casual and very stylish, dimly lit interior, youngish and often noisy crowd, wall-to-wall dance music, stainless steel bar, excellent service, delicious food including mouth-watering soups (most under $6) and a range of glorious 'design-your-own-meal' wok-tossed creations, some Japanese influenced dishes, very busy.

Patee Thai, 73 Fitzroy Street, ph 9534 6839 - small and cosy, cheap and tasty food.

Italian

Café Di Stasio, 31 Fitzroy Street, ph 9525 3999 - huge reputation, excellent food that is often diminished by flamboyant or indifferent service, supreme wine list, very expensive but good lunch specials for under $20, packs them in so tightly it's often impossible not to listen to the next tables conversations.

Leo's Spaghetti Bar, 55 Fitzroy St, ph 9534 5026 - still going strong after 40 years, budget staple for locals, regulars will tell you the brickwork out front spells 'LEO' (and it does!), good pasta dishes, granita coffee and snacks.

Bortolottos, 6 Fitzroy Street, ph 9525 4066 - good traditional fare, sunny atmosphere, quite pricey.

Topolinos, 87 Fitzroy Street, ph 9534 4856 - usually packed with hungry punters ordering cheap and huge servings of pasta and pizza.

Café a Taglio, 157 Fitzroy Street, ph 9534 1344 - yummy takeaway pizza, simple and clean-flavoured toppings, great packaging.

Tolarno Bar and Bistro, 42 Fitzroy Street, ph 9525 5477 - great range of regional food, excellent and filling burgers for around $6.

Chichios, 109 Fitzroy Street, ph 9534 9439 - backpacker specials, cheap pasta, pizza and salads (most under $6), good value.

Cicciolina, 130 Acland Street, ph 9525 3333 (no bookings by telephone) - lively setting with a theatrical feel, often brilliant food (check out the blackboard specials), good wines, spot the TV personalities.

International and Contemporary

Melbourne Wine Room, George Hotel, 125 Fitzroy Street, ph 9525 5599 - sophisticated food and clientele (bar and restaurant menu), modern setting dominated by cliffs of wine racks, focus on superb Victorian wines (over 400 labels), some of the best service in the city, the kind of pad a *Goodfellas* hitman would be proud to call his own, surprisingly inexpensive.

One Fitzroy Street, 1 Fitzroy Street, ph 9593 8800 - modern and sleek decor (grey and white tones predominate) designed by Nonda Katsilidas, downstairs café with upstairs restaurant, hearty meals plus good cheese selection, extensive wine list, fantastic bay views, very popular so get there early, okay prices.

Atlantic, 54 Fitzroy Street, ph 9534 9699 - spacious downstairs bistro and peaceful upstairs restaurant, often appallingly slow service, good focaccias and soups, live jazz most days (upstairs), inexpensive.

Madame Joe Joe, 9 Fitzroy Street, ph 9534 0000 - St Kilda favourite, superb though pricey food (the best deal is the lunch special of two courses, wine and coffee for $19.50).

Victory Café, Fitzroy Street, ph 9534 3727 - located in the former St Kilda Railway Station, has the best coffee and focaccia south of the Yarra River, good breakfasts, lovely pastries, fantastic and friendly service, excellent value.

Bar Ninety Seven, 97 Fitzroy Street, ph 9525 5922 - hangout for the hip and stupendously groovy, innovative and affordable food (though quality is often patchy), inviting and comfortable atmosphere.

Veludo, 175 Acland Street, ph 9534 4456 - upstairs from the bar/café, big choice of fairly pricey mains (duck, veal, tuna, etc), very rich desserts, extensive wine list, casual and unfussy service, non-smokers beware.

Scheherezade, 99 Acland Street, ph 9534 2722 - original clients were mostly Jewish Holocaust survivors but the establishment now attracts a more diverse crowd, authentic servings of traditional European nosh such as goulash, borscht and cheese blintzes, not too pricey.

Galleon Café, 9 Carlisle Street, ph 9534 8934 - funky budget favourite and mainstay for local students and lovers of restaurant kitsch, hearty and healthy fare, good snacks and desserts.

Dogs Bar, 54 Acland Street, ph 9525 3999 - trendy restaurant-cum-watering hole filled with greying pony-tailed men, good food and wine list, inexpensive.

Espresso Bar, 189 Acland Street, ph 9534 8884 - seriously cool café with traditional Italian cream-filled donuts, a wide range of pies and good coffee, always busy.

Balas Café, 1d Shakespeare Grove, ph 9534 6116 - simple but diverse range of Asian food that can be eaten in or taken out, delicious lassi drinks, cheap and incredibly popular (express meals are $4.50).

Big Mouth, 201 Barkly Street, ph 9534 4611 - restaurant that was formerly an upstairs dance studio, huge space, attractive and inexpensive food, top views, newly opened café downstairs.

Momus, 204 Barkly Street, ph 9537 0900 - newly opened, modern and elegant interior, nice service provided by a bevy of black-clad waiters, descriptive and reasonably priced menu, smart wine list, one of the city's few restaurants that accommodates dogs.

Wild Rice, 211 Barkly Street, ph 9534 2849 - specialist 'wholefood' cuisine, all servings free of sugar, dairy and animal products, nice music and helpful fresh-faced staff, inexpensive.

Kiosk, St Kilda Pier, ph 9525 3198 - ideal place for families, fish 'n chips ($7.50) and fantastic city views.

The Stokehouse, 30 Jacka Boulevard, ph 9525 5555 - gorgeous building that was once a teahouse at the turn of the century, expensive restaurant upstairs with cheaper bistro downstairs, food of an exceptionally high standard, sweeping balconies, great views of the bay, always busy.

The Pavilion, 40 Jacka Boulevard, ph 9534 82211 - more outstanding views and good food (especially the seafood), one of the best places in the city to people watch, formerly *Jean Jacques by the Sea*.

The Beach House, 67a Ormond Esplanade, ph 9531 7788 - popular weekend hangout for families and their dogs, lots of eggs, muffins and pastries.

Turtle Café, 34 Glenhuntly Road, Elwood, ph 9525 6952 - basic snacks and excellent coffee, can get busy.

The Elwood Village Grocery, 163 Ormond Road, Elwood, ph 9525 6554 - somewhat off the bitten track, mouth-watering pastries and snacks plus range of old favourites such as bacon and egg pie, good breakfasts and coffee, offensively cheap, highly recommended.

Sails on the Bay, 15 Elwood Foreshore, Elwood, ph 9525 6933 - close to Luna Park, great location overlooking beach, superb wine list, very popular come lunchtime with the Brighton crowd.

Spanish

Café Barcelona, 25 Fitzroy Street, ph 9525 4244 - choose from over 20 tapas plus paella and rosé by the glass, formerly *Diners de Gala*.

Williamstown

Siren, The Beach Pavilion, Esplanade, ph 9397 7811 - the best eatery in the area, sweeping wooden deck offers marvellous sea views, both indoor and outdoor eating, often esoteric menu list but scrumptious desserts, excellent service and ambience, quite pricey.

Moveable Feast

The maroon-coloured *Colonial Tramcar Restaurant* is the worlds only tramcar restaurant operating on a city route. While the food is somewhat predictable and very expensive ($80 a head) the experience is often an interesting one. Reservations for lunch, pre-theatre and dinner services can be made by calling 9696 4000.

Trams can also be hired for dinner functions, parties and special occasions. Half day/ full day hire is around $400/650. For more information contact the Met Information Centre.

Fast Food

The restaurant of choice for most Melburnians is undoubtedly McDonalds. Its hardly surprising then that the ubiquitous Golden Arches are scattered everywhere throughout the city and suburbs. Theres also a glut of KFCs, Pizza Huts and Hungry Jacks as well as Asian, Greek and Lebanese takeaways where fast-food devotees can eat surprisingly well for next to nothing.

Meat pies, sausage rolls, toasted sandwiches, milk shakes as well as a range of specialty foods can be bought from local milk bars, bakeries and delis.

Self Catering

Melbourne is renowned for its fresh produce and wealth of markets and food stores. These include:

Queen Victoria Market, cnr Victoria and Peel Streets, City - a Melbourne shopping icon that is more than a century old, over six hectares of stalls selling everything from lamb kidneys and tongues to pumpkins and potatoes. Stimulating not in sense but in senses as it is highly apt for being seen, heard, touched, tasted and smelled, open Tuesday and Thursday 6am-3pm, Friday 6am-6pm, Saturday 6am-3pm, and Sunday 9am-4pm.

Lygon Food Store, 263 Lygon Street, Carlton, ph 9347 6279 - home of the city's best salami and prosciutto, fabulous Italian, French and Australian cheeses, cured and preserved vegetables, sauces and condiments, good breads and pastries.

King and Godfree, 293 Lygon Street, Carlton. ph 9347 1619 - charming and friendly environment, great deli showcasing pasta, cheeses, small meats and sauces, biscuits and crackers galore, superb range of Australian and imported wines, reasonable prices.

Prahran Market, Commercial Road, Prahran - good produce with an increasing emphasis on Asian foods, fantastic breads and cheeses, fishmongers and poultry specialists, arcade filled with delis, plenty of cafés at edge of market but hard to find a decent coffee, small children's area featuring train rides and merry-go-round, variety and standards have slipped in recent years.

Fiji Produce Shop, 184 Barkly Street, St Kilda, ph 90534 2879 - exotic fruit and vegetables such as taro, cassava and paw-paw, open Monday to Friday 10am-5pm, and Saturday to Sunday 10am-4pm.

Night Life

Melbourne's appetite for all things cultural is reflected in a full performance calendar of opera, ballet, comedy, cinema, live music and theatre. Such diversity has spawned a network of major venues, and even led *Variety*, the international weekly entertainment newspaper, to spotlight the city in its 'Entertainment Town' series - only London, New York and Miami have been awarded a similar honour.

For a complete rundown on what's going on in Melbourne, check the Entertainment Guide (EG) in Fridays edition of *The Age*. Two free newspapers - *Inpress* and *Beat* - also cover a slew of up-and-coming events and are available from record shops, pubs, cafés and venues.

Bookings for general events can be arranged by calling BASS Victoria, ph 11 500 (for theatre and arts events call 11 566, and 11 522 for sports events). You can also buy tickets at a number of BASS outlets located throughout the city centre including the Victorian Arts Centre, Myer and Centrepoint. Agencies are open Monday to Saturday 9am-9pm, and Sunday 10am-5pm.

Discounted tickets are available at Half Tix, Bourke Street Mall, ph 9650 9420. While tickets are substantially reduced, they can only be purchased on the day of performance and paid for in cash. Opening hours are Monday 10am-2pm, Tuesday to Thursday 11am-6pm, Friday 11am-6.30pm, and Saturday 10am-2pm.

Pubs and Live Venues

Melburnians watch more rock concerts than any other city dwellers in Australia. Much of their enthusiasm is due to the city's wealth of major venues which include the National Tennis Centre, the Melbourne Concert Hall at the Victorian Arts Centre, the Sports and Entertainment Centre, The Palace, Lower Esplanade, St Kilda, ph 9534 0655 and the stately Palais Theatre, Lower Esplanade, St

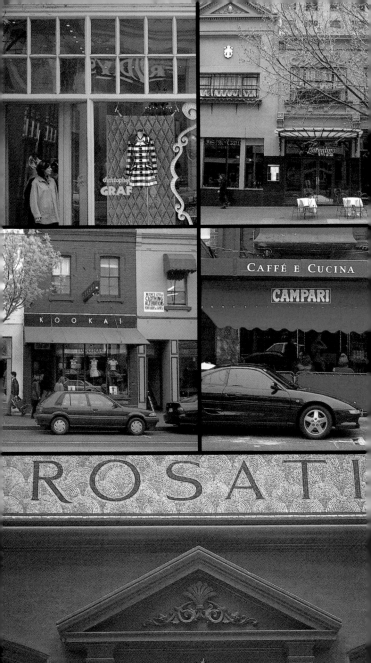

Kilda, ph 9534 0651.

Another reason is that the city is the home of Mushroom Records - the internationally successful indie label that nurtured the careers of Split Enz, Skyhooks and a youthful Nick Cave - plus a number of leading popular music promoters including Paul Dainty, Premier Artists and Frontier Touring Co who brought Madonna, REM, Pearl Jam, David Bowie and Diana Ross to these shores.

A thriving live scene has also led many acts to spearhead a city-based music drive aimed at national and overseas recognition. Successful local artists include mainstream performers Tina Arena, John Farnham and Kate Ceberano, as well as more alternative discoveries Frente!, Not Drowning Waving (and its offshoot My Friend the Chocolate Cake), Tongan-born sister act Vicka and Linda Bull, Rebecca's Empire, Meryl Bainbridge, Dave Graney 'n the Coral Snakes, Hunters and Collectors, Things of Stone and Wood, Paul Kelly and Chris Wilson.

The following are some of the best pubs/venues for catching local and international music:

Lounge, 243 Swanston Street, City, ph 9663 2916 - frothy and popular hangout for hipsters in large lapels, pant suits and Mum's diamantes, often exhilarating range of indigenous, funk and jazz-tinged groups.

Public Bar Hotel, 238 Victoria Street, North Melbourne, ph 9329 6522 - sepulchral front bar, small stage & ulcerating live bands, the marvellous Chris Wilson often headlines.

Rainbow Hotel, 27 St David Street, Fitzroy, ph 9419 4193 - R&B haunt much loved by strapping types with big tatts and embossed jackets, free entry.

Evelyn Hotel, 351 Brunswick Street, Fitzroy, ph 9419 5500 - Melbourne institution noted for its indie thrash bands, florid colours and sharp corners, thrown here and there are pool tables and grungy table and chairs, when the pace slackens go outside and share a post-violence cigarette.

Punters Club Hotel, 376 Brunswick Street, Fitzroy, ph 9417 3006 - one of the oldest sanctums of live music in the city

(Overleaf) Luna Park's distinctive laughing-face entrance.

(Facing) Chapel Street, funky thoroughfare for the young and nimble-figured.

(gigs seven nights a week), marvel at its lager-coloured interior, tottery patrons and hackneyed bands, perfect!

Dan O'Connell Hotel, 225 Canning Street, Carlton, ph 9347 1502 - folksy Irish bands, poetry readings, impromptu stand-up comedy and pub theatre, punters come to talk a streak and drink a lake.

Corner Hotel, 57 Swan Street, Richmond, ph 9427 7300 - small and stygian grunge enclave, always good for its arresting clientele - everything from punks with porcupined hair to patina-faced yuppies braying loudly into their portable phones.

Cherry Tree Hotel, 53 Balmain Street, Richmond, ph 9428 5743 - a bristle of grunge and indie bands.

Molly Blooms Hotel, cnr Bay and Rouse Streets, Port Melbourne, ph 9646 2681 - loads of Irish music and genuine Irish stout.

Continental Café, 134 Greville Street, Prahran, ph 9510 2788 - upstairs from the restaurant, disarmingly chic and dimly lit, one of the standout venues in the city, eclectic sounds ranging from gospel to hip-hop swingbeat, *the* place to see soloists Steven Cummings and Chris Wilson plus incomparable guitarist Shane O'Mara.

Esplanade Hotel, 11 Upper Esplanade, St Kilda, ph 9534 0211 - cavernous venue of beer-soaked carpets, pool tables, pinball machines and great grub at the back kitchen, showcases the crop of local bands, perfect location for whiling away late afternoons watching the sun set or reminiscing with gravelly-voiced diggers, when it gets too hot you can cool off in the bay across the road, should not be missed.

Prince of Wales, 29 Fitzroy Street, St Kilda, ph 9534 8351 - much-missed live venue that once hosted a dazzling array of local and international touring acts, its unabashedly tacky decor (the spew-stained carpets have now entered folklore) is currently being spruced up, ultimately earmarked as (horror of horrors!) a boutique hotel, watch this space for further developments.

Bars

Young and Jacksons, 1 Swanston Street, City, ph 9650 3884 - easily the city's most famous public house, colourful upstairs and downstairs bars, pool tables and the odd pokey machine, site of *Chloe*, a painting of a pneumatic nude that scandalised the city when it was first displayed at the 1880 Great Exhibition.

Emikos Karaoke Bar, 231 Exhibition Street, City, ph 9663 1224 - popular haunt for city executives and foreign businessmen out to make complete fools of themselves, great fun late at night.

JJ's Champagne Bar, Crown Casino complex, ph 9292 6891 - one for the big spenders, take your winnings and indulge in caviar and champagne.

DeOliveiras, 344 Nicholson Street, Fitzroy, ph 9419 1857 - classy and romantic establishment, lavish dining room, European style, with leafy courtyard and very lethal martinis and schnappes, expert service.

Builder Arms Hotel, 211 Gertrude Street, Fitzroy, ph 9419 0818 - stylish local for inner-city playthings, good music.

Gowing Grace Darling, 114 Smith Street, Collingwood, ph 9416 0055 - comfortable, quaint and very roomy, great beer and wines, good food.

The Tote Hotel, 71 Johnston Street, Collingwood, ph 9419 5320 - hardly lustrous front bar boasts the city's best and loudest jukebox that features everything from Iggy Pop to the Smashing Pumpkins, order a drink then crank it up.

Jazz

Jazz features heavily at a number of Melbourne's nightspots including the Bridge, Rainbow, Evelyn and Esplanade hotels, as well as the Hotel Como, Novotel, Lounge and upstairs at the Atlantic restaurant. Venues specifically catering to jazz include:

Bennetts Lane Jazz Club, 25 Bennetts Lane, City, ph 9663 2856 - undoubtedly one of the country's best and most sophisticated jazz venues, small and smoky with hankie-sized tables, convivial atmosphere, features the very best of local and overseas combos and soloists (Wynton Marsalis, Harry Connick Jnr), hibiscus shirts are a must.

Jazz Lane, 390 Lonsdale Street, City, ph 9670 5550 - newly opened, good acts and service, very comfortable.

Theatre

According to Melbourne folklore, local theatre burgeoned due to the atrocious weather which meant writers, directors, actors and manqués were forced indoors to pursue their artistic endeavours. Whether there is a grain of truth in this is neither here nor there - the fact remains that the city's reputation as the theatre capital of Australia is beyond dispute. Melbourne is currently experiencing a boom in theatre production, the quality of stage product continues to rise (prompting a pleased Premier Kennett to compare the city's theatre as every bit as good as Broadway or London), while increasingly more venues are being restored to their former glory.

Melbournes major venues for theatre include:

The Victorian Arts Centre, 100 St Kilda Road, Southgate, ph 9281 8000 - enormous multi-venue complex that is the largest in Australia, comprises the State Theatre (capacity over 2000), the Playhouse (capacity 900) and the smallish George Fairfax Studio (capacity 430), also includes the National Gallery of Victoria, the Melbourne Concert Hall (capacity 2700) & the Sidney Myer Music Bowl (capacity 12,000), hosts opera, musicals, drama, ballet and concerts.

The Regent, 191 Collins Street, City, ph 9299 9500 - recently resuscitated after being boarded up and neglected for 26 years. Over 500 crafts people worked to faithfully recreate and remodel the interior which includes grand ballrooms, a magnificent chandelier and a one-tonne Wurlitzer organ, capacity 2000, opulent and amazing theatrical building that ranks as one of the best in the world, features big-budget and high-grossing productions (The Regent was recently home to Andrew Lloyd Weber's *Sunset Boulevard*).

Princess Theatre, 163 Spring Street, City, ph 9663 3300 - lovely and elaborate 19th century building boasting a trumpeting angel at its centre, the site is believed to be haunted by the actor Federeci. Recently refurbished, showcases international blockbusters of the *Les Miserables*, *The Phantom of the Opera*, and *Beauty and the Beast* ilk.

Forum Melbourne, cnr Flinders and Russell Streets, City, ph 9650 3033 - built in 1929 and recently transformed into a stylish cabaret-cum-theatre, distinctive twin-domed exterior, capacity 850, some stand-up comedy, formerly The Old State Theatre.

Her Majestys Theatre, 219 Exhibition Street, City, ph 9663 3211 - built in 1866 and lovingly restored, capacity 1600, features mostly musicals and Broadway hits.

Athenaeum, 188 Collins Street, City, ph 9650 3504 - predominantly drama and Shakespearian plays.

Comedy Theatre, 240 Exhibition Street, City, ph 9242 1000 - plans to renovate, capacity 800.

National Theatre, cnr Carlisle and Barkly Streets, St Kilda, ph 9534 0221 - theatre performances, music concerts, film and comedy festivals.

Melbournes theatre companies include:

Melbourne Theatre Company (MTC), 129 Ferrars Street, South Melbourne, ph 96864000 - government funded, the country's oldest surviving theatrical company, stages brash and often controversial Australian works (everything from Ray Lawlers *The Summer of the Seventeenth Doll* to David Williamsons *The Heretic*), Shakespeare and overseas adaptations, displays the best of local dramatic talent, most of the company's major productions are staged at the Victorian Arts Centre.

Playbox Theatre Company, Malthouse Theatre Complex, 113 Sturt Street, South Melbourne, ph 9685 5111 - founded in 1976, outstanding venue that was once a grain warehouse, two theatres plus bar and restaurant, produces 100% contemporary Australian works, showcases the country's best playwrights and dramaturgists (David Williamson, Louis Nowra, Nick Enright, Joanna Murray-Smith).

Theatreworks, 14 Acland Street, St Kilda, ph 9534 4879 - innovative productions.

La Mama Theatre, 205 Faraday Street, Carlton, ph 9347 6142 - small but excellent venue for up-and-coming Australian talent.

Comedy

Melbourne's status as the comedy capital of Australia is richly deserved. The city has produced a bank of comedic talent over the years including Barry Humphries, Steve

Vizard, Michael Veitch, Tracey Harvey, Wendy Harmer, Rob Sitch, Santo Cilauro, John Clarke, double act Matt Parkinson and Matt Quartermaine, Judith Lucy, Anthony Morgan and Greg Fleet. A visit during the Melbourne International Comedy Festival (see the Festivals chapter) is a must for stomach-clutchers and potential Rupert Pupkins (the drearily unfunny comedian in Martin Scorceses *The King of Comedy* remember?). Otherwise try the following venues:

The Melbourne Comedy Club, 380 Lygon Street, Carlton, ph 9348 1622.1 *The Last Laugh Theatre Restaurant,* 64 Smith Street, Collingwood, ph 9419 8600 - comedy institution.

Prince Patrick Hotel, 135 Victoria Parade, Collingwood, ph 9419 4197 - small, intimate and sometimes intimidating (especially for the comics) venue, great place for heckling, often features one of Anthony Morgan's funnier shows.

Gershwin Room, Esplanade Hotel, 11 The Upper Esplanade, St Kilda, ph 9534 0211 - fertile breeding ground for some of the country's best comics.

Nightclubs

The city's nightclubs are many and varied. Expect entrance fees ranging from $5-10, strictly enforced dress codes, and legions of bouncers with oak-tree arms.

Warning: Clubs along King Street are notoriously peopled by young drunks and hotheads. Many patrons have been beaten up both inside and outside these establishments, while stabbings and shootings are becoming increasingly commonplace. Some taxi drivers now refuse to work the strip. If you choose to visit the area late at night, make sure you're with a large group. The in-crowd considers showing up before midnight at the following venues an egregious breach of good taste, but who cares what they think anyway:

Metro Nightclub, 20 Bourke Street, City, ph 9663 4288 - Australia's largest nightclub with several architect-designed levels and bars, often crowded venue for the young, the not so young and the moneyed, sounds range from House to Garage to commercial dance tunes, superb location.

The Night Cat, 141 Johnston Street, Fitzroy, ph 9417 0090 -

chintzy decor, spacious and very comfortable, fat funk, acid jazz, heavy dub, Afro-Cuban rhythms and live jam sounds abound.

The Redhead, Aughtie Drive, South Melbourne, ph 9690 7877 - located in one of Melbournes quiet little inglenooks, favoured haunt of starlets, wannabees and incorrigible fashion victims, great sounds supplied by heavily credentialled DJs.

Saratoga Club, 46 Albert Street, South Melbourne, ph 9699 8177 - tries to be purposefully, provocatively cool though the venues hardly the stuff of legend, does spin some of the latest grooves though.

Chasers, 386 Chapel Street, Prahran, ph 9827 6615 - although the club's been around for a long time its still one of the biggest groove beasts in the city, all muscle and workout so come dressed to dance.

Cinema

Pricing wars between Melbourne's main cinema chains now means drastically reduced tickets. Expect to pay only $6.50 at most Village cinemas and around $8-11 elsewhere. Discount tickets are available for concession card holders (students, pensioners, etc) and children. Independent cinemas also have a discount night (usually Monday or Tuesday) when ticket prices tend to be halved. Mainstream cinemas include:

Greater Union Russell Cinemas, 131 Russell Street, City, ph 9654 8133

Hoyts Cinema Centre, 140 Bourke Street, City, ph 9663 3303

Village Centre, 206 Bourke Street, City, ph 9667 6565

Jam Factory 8, 500 Chapel Street, South Yarra, ph 9827 2424 - recently refurbished with a heavy dose of industrial strength nostalgia (life-size mannequins of Elvis Presley and Marilyn Monroe, her skirt billowing around her waist), massive marble foyer, eight-screener that has the most comfortable seating in the city, average choc tops.

Independent cinemas include:

Kino, 45 Collins Place, ph 9650 2100 - easily the best place in the City to view movies, the choc tops are divine.

Chinatown Cinema, 200 Bourke Street, City, ph 9662 3465 -

Chinese features with English subtitles, often has midnight shows.

Lumiere, 108 Lonsdale Street, City, ph 9639 1055 - classics and new-wave releases.

State Film Centre, 1 Macarthur Street, East Melbourne, ph 9651 1515 - advanced screenings, arty and independent releases, runs childrens programs during school holidays.

Cinema Nova, 380 Lygon Street, Carlton, ph 9347 5331 - recently enlarged, great lolly section, very popular.

Capital Theatre, 113 Swanston Street, City, ph 9650 4756 - 600-seater showing quality classics and arthouse films, the Walter Burley Griffin interiors should keep you interested once the subtitles pall.

Carlton Moviehouse, 235 Faraday Street, Carlton, ph 9347 8909 - built in 1909 and the oldest surviving cinema in the inner city, recently classified by the National Trust, student hangout, eat next door at Genevieve's restaurant and get a 10% discount to the movies.

Longford, 59 Toorak Road, South Yarra, ph 9867 2700 - mostly independent releases, smallish but comfortable.

Trak, 445 Toorak Road, Toorak, ph 9827 9333 - small movies, small venue.

Cinema Como, cnr Chapel Street and Toorak Road, ph 9827 7533 - grand setting in an enormous shopping complex, good viewing screen.

Astor Theatre, 1 Chapel St, St Kilda, ph 9510 1414 - art-house, classic and alternative films, fantastic ambience, the front steps are one of the city's popular meeting spots.

George Cinema, 133-37 Fitzroy Street, St Kilda, ph 9534 6922 - recent addition to the city's cinema scene, good seats and lollies, Café Diva next door has cheap and tasty food plus there's a giant screen showing the latest videos.

Valhalla Cinema, 89 High Street, Northcote, ph 9482 2001 - marvellous Art Deco building designed by Walter Burley Griffin that was a Melbourne institution for 20 years. Featured the very best of cult and classic films, its calendar of up-and-coming releases could be seen on every share-house fridge or dunny door, sadly closed its doors and shut down its projectors in 1996, decision yet to be made on what is to be done with the building.

Readings

Poetry and literary readings, music, comedy and night-long gabfests are held at the following:

Arthouse, 616 Elizabeth Street, City, ph 9347 3917.

Lounge, 243 Swanston Street, City, ph 9663 2916.

Evelyn Hotel, 351 Brunswick Street, Fitzroy, ph 9419 5500.

Victorian Writers Centre, 1st Floor, 156 George Street, Fitzroy, ph 9415 1077.

Dan O'Connell Hotel, 225 Canning St, Carlton, ph 9347 1502.

Jimmy Watsons, 333 Lygon Street, Carlton, ph 9347 3985.

Theatreworks, 14 Acland Street, St Kilda, ph 9534 4879.

Gambling

Melbournes *Crown Casino*, opened in 1995, was temporarily stabled at the World Trade Centre building, and quickly became the richest in Australia. (At the time of writing, the casino had attracted over nine million visitors, making it the number one attraction in Victoria.). It was also the country's largest with 130 gaming tables, five restaurants, six bars, over 1200 poker machines ('pokies'), plus several sports betting facilities.

Much of the casinos success could be put down to aggressive advertising and marketing, the venues favourable location close to the heart of Melbourne, and a community - long deprived of roulette wheels, blackjack tables and legal poker games - seeking novelty and new forms of entertainment at every turn.

But success came at a cost. Streets approaching the casino were bedecked with billboards advertising counselling services for addicted gamblers while ominous signs warned parents not to leave their children un-attended in cars (an early legacy that provoked a hurried PR campaign). So much for the casinos slogan that 'everyone's a winner'.

The Crown Casinos new home is now a 14-acre site along the banks of the Yarra River. Opened May 1997, the complex dominates the city centre much like similar venues once dwarfed pre-revolutionary Havana. Its facilities include a ballroom holding 2500 people, a 1000-

seat showroom (already likened to the 'world's biggest bingo hall), an 1800-seat Lyric Theatre, a 14-screen theatre installed by Village Roadshow and running continuously, 40 bars, and 25 restaurants including a Planet Hollywood and an All-Star Café. The casino also harbours a twin-tower five-star hotel with 500 rooms (to be doubled by 1999), various sports and entertainment clubs, a massive undercover car park holding over 5000 vehicles, plus a giant retail promenade featuring Gucci, Prada and DKNY shops. As for gamblers, they have plenty of opportunity to chance their arm as over 2500 pokies and 350 gaming tables have been installed.

Yes, it is stupendously big (the complex is, in fact, the largest building in the country). The casino is also refreshingly bold and adventurous with its 'front-of-shop' pillars belching fire every so often, its cascading fountains, shiny lobbies and sweeping Hollywood-style marble staircases. While some passers-by look on the complex with awe, others, notably the city's middle class and clergy, demonstrate about as much interest as a cow looking at a new gate. Understandably the Crown Casino has polarised most Melburnians but nothing quite like it exists in Australia. That, in itself, is an achievement. Away from the casino, you can have a 'flutter' on the horses (in particular the obligatory bet on the Melbourne Cup run the first Tuesday in November) or dogs. Betting can be done via any city or suburban Totalisator Agency Board (TAB) shop. Another less-expensive option is to simply buy a lottery ticket.

Shopping

Melbourne is awash with department stores, boutique and specialty shops, and everywhere you look you can find designer clothes, jewellery, toys, books, electronic gadgets, oddities and knick-knackery.

A trip into the heart of Melbourne will reveal a sometimes unfathomable conundrum of elevated walk ways and interlinked shops daring you to crack their extraordinary codes. There are major department stores such as Myers, 314 Bourke Street Mall, and David Jones, 310 Bourke Street Mall, selling everything from clothing to cosmetics and homeware to haberdashery; vast shopping arcades including Australia on Collins, Collins Place, Sportsgirl Centre and the opulent Block Arcade (once a popular promenade for the ostentatious aristos of old) where you can trawl hundreds of fashion, food and specialty shops; and Collins Street, a Parisian-style boulevard crammed with fashionable boutiques displaying Chanel, Hermes, Yves Saint Laurent, Armani and the utility-obsessed designs of Prada.

But most spectacular (and bewildering) of them all is the futuristic Melbourne Central shopping complex, on the corner of La Trobe and Elizabeth Streets. Opened in 1991 and spread over two city blocks, this 55-level tower houses over 200 shops of every persuasion, plus restaurants and eateries by the score. Dominating the centre of the complex is an enormous cone-shaped dome enclosing the brick Shot Tower (1870), which has been classified by the National Trust.

Melbourne is also a bargain hunters paradise with factory outlets for most city-based fashion labels. Tours to some of the city's largest factories and warehouses (with lunch thrown in) can be arranged through Shopping Spree Tours, ph 9596 6600 and Melbourne Shopping Tours, ph 9416 3722. Otherwise spend your time scouring the areas of Richmond, Fairfield, Bentleigh, Collingwood,

Fitzroy and Brunswick.

Two comprehensive and definitive publications for bargain shoppers are *The Bargain Shoppers Guide to Melbourne* ($7.95) and *Pam's Guide to Discount Melbourne* ($12.95). The latter has 320 pages of upmarket to flea-market purchases, plus handy tips and information. Both are available at most newsagents and bookstores.

Clothing and Jewellery

Melburnians spend an inordinate amount of money on clothing and accessories, and feel most comfortable when wearing black (white hardly looks good when you don't have a tan). They usually gravitate to major department stores and specialty shops in the city centre, Southgate and the Crown Casino complex, or along certain suburban strips such as Chapel Street in South Yarra. A fanfare of fashionable shops includes:

Cose Ipanema, 113 Collins Street, ph 9650 3457 - stocks up-to-the-minute clothing from fab designers such as Romeo Giglio and Dolce e Gabbana.

Makers Mark Gallery, Shop 9, 101 Collins Street, City, ph 9654 8488 - designer jewellery including earrings, cufflinks and brooches.

The Hermes Paris Shop, Grand Hyatt Plaza, 123 Collins Street, City, ph 9654 5552 - exquisite and very expensive gifts, great scarves and shawls.

Coogi Connections, 86 Collins Street, City, ph 9650 4407 - artistic and distinctively colourful knitwear for all ages.

Australian Way, Shop 214-216, 260 Collins Street, City, ph 9654 3021 - Australian clothing, Aboriginal art, souvenirs and giftware.

Dangerfield, 224 Flinders Street, City, ph 9654 1759 - colourful and very catchy shirts, trousers, caps, jackets and jewellery, excellent prices.

Succhi, 107 Melbourne Central, 300 Lonsdale Street, City, ph 9663 5478 - popular retail branch selling shoes for men and women, often has the highly coveted Patrick Cox range in stock.

Sam Bear, 225 Russell Street, City, ph 9663 2191 - outdoor and long-lasting clothing, stockists of Hard Yakka workwear.

RM Williams, Shop 229, Melbourne Central, 300 Lonsdale St, ph 9663 7126 - legendary Australian outfitter, tough and durable jackets, shirts, moleskin trousers and boots.

Stephen Davies, 65 Gertrude Street, Fitzroy, ph 9419 6296 - lovely handmade shoes, prices start from around $300.

Scally and Trombone, 313 Brunswick St, Fitzroy, ph 9419 6038 - up-to-the-minute & inexpensive hats and jewellery.

The Dime Store, 33 Bridge Road, Richmond, ph 9428 8434 - good range of casual womens streetwear and seconds from independent designer shops.

It Inc, 157-9 Greville Street, Prahran, ph 9521 1955 - funky clothing, jewellery and homeware.

Morrisey Edmiston, 549 Chapel Street, South Yarra, ph 9824 0582 - Australia's leading designers, clothing for wannabees, rocksters and hipsters, their twice annual sales (up to 75% off most goods) are compulsory.

Scanlan and Theodore, 539 Chapel Street, South Yarra, ph 9827 2449 - exclusive and finely detailed womens wear.

Calibre, 457 Chapel Street, South Yarra, ph 9826 4394 - trendy menswear clothier, great ties, belts and shoes.

Country Road, cnr Chapel Street and Toorak Road, South Yarra, ph 9824 0133 - multi-level concept store of fashion and accessories for men and women, excellent basics plus okay prices.

Mooks, 491 Chapel Street, South Yarra, ph 9827 9966 - hip streetwear for men and women.

Bracewell, 450 Chapel Street, South Yarra, ph 9827 1420 - top imported fashion including Paul Smith.

Marcs, 459 Chapel St, South Yarra, ph 9827 5290 - fashionable menswear, good sales, expensive imported shoes.

Saba, 538 and 548 Chapel Street, ph 9824 2937/9827 5250 - commands two stores along fashionable Chapel Street, men and women can choose from a range of swanky suits, shirts and accessories.

Kimberley Smith, 135 Toorak Road, South Yarra, ph 9820 3567 - fashionable costume jewellery, prices range from reasonable to stratospheric.

Seconds, Bargains and Retro

American Rag, Shop 325, Melbourne Central, 300 Lonsdale Street, City, ph 9663 8745 - fantastic imported Champion sweats, bowling shirts, denim and leather jackets, stretch pants and Hanes T-shirts.

Recycle, 433 Bourke Street, City, ph 9670 9997 - local designer labels plus Prada (brilliantly layered fashion for trendy nerds), Chanel, Ermenegildo Zegna and Hugo Boss imports.

Old Modern, 258 Brunswick Street, Fitzroy, ph 9419 1189 - spotlessly presented clothes including vintage Christian Dior suits and dresses.

Dangerfield Factory Outlet, 23 Northumberland Street, Collingwood, ph 9416 3694 - fashionable streetwear, up to 50% off normal retail prices.

Secondo, 286 Toorak Rd, South Yarra, ph 9827 8907 - eye-popping selection of local & imported clothing from Saba and Country Road to Issey Miyake & Dolce e Gabbana.

Best Dressed, 1041 High Street, Armadale, ph 9824 7467 - affordable Armani and Donna Karan dresses, mostly wholesale prices.

Junkarucci, 193 Barkly Street, St Kilda, ph 9525 3224 - funky knick-knacks like 1960s leather school bags, feather boas, chunky platform shoes and Stussy bags.

Opals

Altmann and Cherry, 120 Exhibition Street, City, ph 9650 9685 - Melbourne's largest opal showroom with an expansive range of opals from inexpensive gifts to treasured heirlooms, displays the largest and most valuable gem opal in the world valued at US$1,800,000.

Ashley Opals, 85 Collins Street, City, ph 9654 4866 - another enormous selection of opals, plus jewellery, souvenirs and leather accessories.

Andrew Cody Opals, Showroom 1/119 Swanston St, City, ph 9654 5533 - shop outfitted to resemble an opal mine, highly prized collection including the rare black opal.

Aboriginal Art

Kimberley Art, 76 Flinders Lane, City, ph 9654 5890 - one of the city's most important galleries for Aboriginal art, supplies museum-quality works from north and central Australia to domestic as well as international collectors, also has an excellent consultancy service.

Aboriginal Gallery of Dreamings, 73-77 Bourke Street, City, ph 9650 3277 - consistently good collection of indigenous fine art.

Aboriginal Handicrafts, Century Building, 9th Floor, 125-33 Swanston Street, City, ph 9650 4717 - hand-crafted artefacts including boomerangs, didgeridoos, carvings, bark paintings and woven baskets.

Antiques

Graham Geddes Antiques, 877 High Street, Armadale, ph 9509 0308 - the country's largest antique business (the owner shed goods worth over $2 million in late 1996 to downsize operations) with a fantastic international reputation, great selection of antiques and antiquities from around the world, specialises in Italian ceramics, reproductions also available.

Antique Decor, 899 High Street, Armadale, ph 9509 7322 - antique lighting specialists, importers of quality sculpture and decorative arts.

Park Lane Antique Centre, 1170 High Street, Armadale, ph 9500 9718 - over 30 dealers showcasing antique furniture and chinaware.

Martin of Melbourne, 1044 High Street, Armadale, ph 9509 3444 - antique and estate fine jewellery.

Chapel Street Bazaar, 217 Chapel Street, Prahran, ph 9529 1727 - collectables and memorabilia, good Art Deco pieces including Bakelite lamps,old tools & scientific equipment.

Kazari Japanese Interiors, 533 Chapel Street, South Yarra, ph 9826 8472 - antique chests of drawers, tables and curios.

Grey Street Bazaar, 127 Grey Street, St Kilda, ph 9525 5770 - antiques, 1950s-1970s collectables, and Art Deco bric-a-brac.

Art Galleries

Metropolitan Melbourne currently boasts over 200 public and commercial galleries including:

Anna Schwartz, 185 Flinders Lane, City, ph 9654 6131 - undeniably *the* leading commercial gallery in Melbourne, understated in approach with painting and sculpture by many contemporary artists working in a minimalist and conceptualist mode, very cutting edge.

Tribal Art Gallery, 103 Flinders Lane, City, ph 9650 4186 - fine collection of traditional and contemporary Melanesian sculpture in wood, clay and wickerwork.

200 Gertrude Street, 200 Gertrude Street, Fitzroy, ph 9419 3406 - three gallery spaces and 18 artists studios (including two for interstate and international artists), extensive program of exhibitions, seminars, lectures and events, good focus on experimental and innovative works by local and overseas artists.

Tolarno Galleries, 121 Victoria Street, Fitzroy, ph 9419 2121 - eclectic range by artists working in more traditional forms, often features some excellent architectural works.

Handicrafts

The Meat Market Craft Centre, 42 Courtney Street, North Melbourne, ph 9329 9966 - for over 90 years the site of Melbourne's wholesale meat market and now one of the country's best craft centres with exhibitions of contemporary crafts (held in the famous Main Hall featuring a marvellous barrel-vault ceiling), accessible workshop allows visitors to observe cratftspeople modelling glass, textile, ceramic and wood, open Tuesday to Sunday 10am-5pm.

Collins Place Arts and Craft Market, 45 Collins Street, City, ph 018 88 2018 - over 130 stalls of Australian handicrafts.

Bookshops

Melburnians pride themselves on being booksy people. The city has the highest readership of books, newspapers, periodicals and magazines in Australia, as well as the largest concentration of bookshops in the country. Titles on gardening (naturally), football or anything written by a local author consistently ride high on the best-seller lists.

The city's flagship bookshop chains are Angus and

(Facing page) Entrance to Queen Victoria Market, Australia's largest with over 1000 stalls [Top left]. The Italianate-style Melbourne City Baths [Top right]. Melbourne's distinctiove, rambling functional trams (plus a former means of transport) [Middle right]. A detail of RMIT's award-winning though daffy facade [Middle left]. Fruit stalls provide a detonation of colour in the city's streets [Bottom].

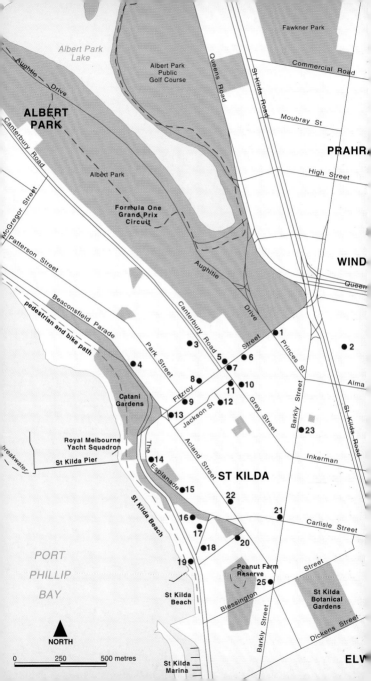

MAP KEY
ST KILDA MAP

Accomodation

1. Ritz Backpackers
2. Charnwood Motor Inn
3. Victoria House B&B
4. Robinsons by the Sea
10. St Kilda Coffee Palace
    Backpackers Inn
11. Leopard House
12. Enfield House
    Backpackers
15. Novotel Bayside
    Melbourne
23. Olembia Guesthouse

Other

6. George Cinema
13. Prince of Wales Hotel
14. Esplanade Hotel
16. The Palace
17. Palais Theatre
18. Luna Park
21. National Theatre
24. St Kilda Town Hall

Eating

5. Victory Café
7. Melbourne Wine Room
8. Tolarno Bar and Bistro
9. Leos Spaghetti Bar
19. The Pavilion
20. Balas Café
22. Dogs Bar
25. Wild Rice

Robertson Bookworld, cnr Bourke and Elizabeth Streets, ph 9670 8861, Collins Booksellers, 115 Elizabeth Street, ph 9602 3949, and Reader's Feast (formerly a Dymocks franchise), cnr Bourke and Swanston Streets, ph 9663 4699. Each has well-stocked sections with thousands of titles to choose from and lots of armchairs for relaxed browsing. They also have a number of branches scattered throughout the city and suburbs.

Other good shops include:

Foreign Language Bookshop, 259 Collins Street, City, ph 9654 2883 - fiction, language-learning kits, dictionaries, guidebooks and maps.

Page One, 179 Collins Street, City, ph 9654 3886 - excellent source of visual magazines and books, worth a visit just to see the trendy interior - architects, interior design market.

Technical Book and Magazine Company, 295 Swanston Street, City, ph 9663 3951 - technical, specialist and general books.

Whole Earth Bookshop, 246 Swanston Street, City, ph 9662 3431 - general and alternative titles.

Hill of Content, 86 Bourke Street, City, ph 9662 9472 - opened in 1922 and still going strong, fabulous general bookstore with first-rate classics, cookery, travel, biography and non-fiction sections, some international magazines and newspapers, desperately needs some chairs for sitting and reading.

Minotaur, 220 Bourke Street, City, ph 9639 1144 - city's leading retailer of comics, sci-fi, fantasy and horror.

Map Lands, 372 Little Bourke Street, City, ph 9670 4383 - houses one of Australia's most extensive collections of travel guidebooks, atlases, globes, travel kits, etc, formerly Bowyangs Maps and Travel Guides.

McGills, 187 Elizabeth Street, City, ph 9602 5566 - specialists in general and technical titles, big range of national and overseas newspapers and magazines.

Mary Martin, Ground Floor, Southgate, ph 9699 2292 - good selection of fiction and trade titles.

Brunswick Street Bookstore, 305 Brunswick Street, Fitzroy, ph 9416 1030 - contemporary and classic books, big range of magazines, big comfy chairs, open late.

Readings, 338 Lygon Street, Carlton, ph 9347 6633 - kingpin of the Readings city-wide chain, comprehensive general fiction and specialist (philosophy, politics, history, cultural studies, etc) section, good children's books, great international magazines, Foucault, Derrida, Lacan *et les autres* T-shirts hang from the ceiling, interesting choice of books on the selection tables, front window plastered with room-rental ads, can order in.

Small Print, 420 Rathdowne Street, Carlton, ph 9347 9997 - childrens books and tapes, excellent new titles.

Emerald Hill Bookshop, 336 Clarendon Street, South Melbourne, ph 9699 5966 - titles ranging from art and advertising to children and cooking.

Kill City, 126 Greville Street, Prahran, ph 9510 6661 - specialists in hard-boiled crime fiction with an excellent range of magazines, mail-order service, great T-shirts with shop logo on the front.

Books in Print, 100 Glenferrie Road, Malvern Vic ph 9500 9631 has an excellent range of new releases and backlist.

Hares and Hyenas, 135 Commercial Road, South Yarra, ph 9824 0110 - alternative titles.

Chronicles, 91 Fitzroy Street, St Kilda, ph 9537 2677 - smallish retailer with latest titles plus old favourites.

Cosmos, 112 Acland Street, St Kilda, ph 9525 3852 - shelves filled with recent releases, biographies, classics, philosophy and history plus there's a world, jazz and popular CDs collection at the rear.

Metropolis, 160 Acland Street, St Kilda, ph 9525 4866 - recently opened Cosmos offshoot specialising mostly in titles with an arts, cinema and music theme.

Music

Blockbuster Music, 152 Bourke Street, City, ph 9663 5277 - city flagship with huge selection of the latest mainstream CDs, cassettes and accessories.

Gaslight, 85 Bourke Street, City, ph 9650 9009 - hard-to-find collectables plus music videos.

Au Go Go, 349 Little Bourke Street, City, ph 9670 0677 - tiny establishment that crams oodles of CDs, tapes and records into two floors, great selection of new releases plus collectables, music books & magazines also for sale.

Discurio, 105 Elizabeth Street, City, ph 9600 1488 - brand-spanking new premises, the city's best range of jazz, R&B, soul, world, country and classical music.

Blue Moon, 30 Johnston Street, Fitzroy, ph 9415 1157 - good collection of world music, jazz and reggae.

Readings Music, 366 Lygon Street, Carlton, ph 9347 7473 - excellently priced popular music plus great coverage of golden oldies, collectables, jazz, folk, world, blues, country and soundtracks, also has twice yearly sales of the biggest and best range of classical music, music books and magazines for sale.

Raoul Records, 166 Acland Street, St Kilda, ph 9525 5066 - excellent jazz, hip hop, house, ambient, soul and R&B collection, music books and magazines for sale.

Markets

Queen Victoria Market, cnr Victoria and Peel Streets, City - originally the site of Melbourne's first official cemetery in

1837 until more than 10,000 remains were moved 80 years later to accommodate its new function. Easily the largest outdoor market in Australia with more than 1000 stalls selling everything from lambs' tongues to stuffed koalas. Attracts more than 2.5 million visitors annually, making it one of the largest tourist attractions in the state (check out the gaggles of tourists around the didgeridoo and boomerang stands). Open Tuesday and Thursday 6am-3pm, Friday 6am-6pm, Saturday 6am-3pm, and Sunday 9am-4pm (when stall-holders sell only clothing and accessories).

Sunday Market, Victorian Arts Centre, 100 St Kilda Road, Southgate - handicrafts, open Sunday 10am-6pm.

South Melbourne Market, cnr York & Coventry Streets, South Melbourne - produce, clothing, handicrafts and homeware, open Wednesday, Friday, Saturday & Sunday.

Greville Street Sunday Market, Greville Street, Prahran - various odds and ends, open Sunday noon-5pm.

Prahran Market, Commercial Road, Prahran - delis, fruit and vegetables plus meat, fish and poultry, open Tuesday, Thursday, Friday & Saturday from dawn until dusk.

Esplanade Art and Craft Market, Upper Esplanade, St Kilda - operating for over 25 years, showcases the endeavours (clothing, hats, accessories, jewellery, paintings, photography, glassware, pottery, kites and candles) of more than 200 local artisans, a lot of junk but does spring the occasional surprise, open Sunday 10am-5pm.

Sightseeing

Melbourne's bank of attractions have probably gathered more laurels and brickbats than any other city in Australia. However cavalier some of their descriptions, they remain an integral part of one of the most graceful cities in the world. At least in this, the visitors who have come successively since its founding, are in agreement. After all, where else can you find a metropolitan history littered with prosperity and upheaval, and a culture the envy of all. Or a city ringed with picture-book parkland (predominantly the work of 19th-century botanic pioneers such as Charles La Trobe and William Guilfoyle) and fabulous stadiums for sport. Or eye-popping skyscrapers and tranquil, terrace-housed streets. Or multi-venue arts complexes and handsome galleries and museums. And where else can you see high-marking footballers one day and a musical production of *Les Miserables* the next. Melbourne has all this, and more.

The majority of sights and attractions covered in this chapter are either in or within walking distance from the city centre, and most are accessible by public transport.

City Centre
Flinders Street Station
The focal point of Melbourne's rail system and an enduring city symbol, Flinders Street Station was first built in 1854 and completed 55 years later. It is the country's oldest metropolitan station and first steam rail terminal, and is now used by over 100,000 Melburnians daily. Extensively remodelled over the years - the last time being 1981, although it has recently been tarted up with a fresh coat of paint - the Federation-style station is a prime meeting place where people gather 'under the clocks' or take in the heady mixture of traffic sounds, bagpipes (from a busker out front) and the bells of St Paul's Cathedral.

Highlights

Parliament House - one of the world's finest examples of Victorian architecture.

State Library and the National Museum of Victoria - trawl through vast collections of books and assorted exhibits.

Old Melbourne Gaol - embark on a nightmarish but fascinating tour.

Southgate - wine, dine, shop and be entertained along the Yarra River.

Victorian Arts Centre - Melbourne's cultural life revolves around this complex, the spire's lighting is one of the greatest engineering feats in Australia's history.

National Gallery of Victoria - houses the country's most important collection of art.

Melbourne Exhibition Centre - massive business facility with an award-winning design.

Melbourne Cricket Ground - Australia's largest and best-known colosseum for watching AFL and cricket matches also has an excellent sporting museum.

Royal Botanic Gardens - landscape gardening at its breathtaking best.

King's Domain - enormous green expanse holding the Shrine of Remembrance and La Trobe's Cottage.

Brunswick, Lygon and Chapel Streets - where to eat, shop and be seen.

Royal Melbourne Zoological Gardens - Australia's oldest zoo with over 350 species of animal.

St Kilda - Melbourne's famous and much-visited seaside community.

Ripponlea - one of Australia's pre-eminent suburban estates.

City Square

Melbourne's most visible and notorious planning failure surely counts as an attraction. Lying between Flinders Lane and Collins Street and opened in 1980, this paved public space is such a monochromatic eyesore that one wag wrote 'even the pigeons think twice before visiting'. Cringing with embarrassment to the front of the square is a statue honouring Burke and Wills, the hapless explorers who set out to cross the continent from south to north in 1860. Loath to take along Aboriginal guides, the pair perished several months into the expedition (one of their party survived only after he accepted the help of local Aborigines along the way). The square is soon to have a makeover with the addition of a hotel, canal and faux European café-style seating but they're hardly the addition's Melburnians have awaited for so long.

Melbourne Town Hall

The Town Hall, on the corner of Swanston and Collins Streets, is one of Melbourne's grandest buildings. Built from Tasmanian stone and completed in 1880 (a grand portico was added seven years later), it has enough interior features to turn most visitors into squinting, purblind myopes. Apart from a clock tower and mansard roof, a main hall (capacity 3000) with a marvellous foyer, libraries, reception and meeting rooms, elaborate murals and plasterwork, bronze chandeliers, Australian timbers, curtains of stained glass windows, and sumptuous toilets too elaborate to discuss, there's also an enormous concert organ that ranks as one of the finest in Australia.

Chinatown

Melbourne's Chinatown, which dates from the 1850s gold rushes, has its epicentre in Little Bourke Street, a thoroughfare filled with restaurants and takeaway Peking Duck shops, artisan galleries, and many attractive old buildings. Far and away the most visited sight in the vicinity is the *Chinese Museum* at 22 Cohen Place, displaying and promoting a history of Chinese experience in Australia. Inside is a trove of cultural treasures, contemporary and permanent exhibitions by local artists, a dynamic interactive display of Chinese sojourners to the country, as well as Dai Loong, reputedly the largest dragon in the world.

 Guided tours of the museum as well as Chinatown are available daily 10am-4.30pm.

The Russell Street Underground

Melbourne's first underground lavatory for both men and women was built in 1902. Its construction was a significant achievement at the time, and drew on the prevailing advances in sanitary and medical knowledge as well as solving the hygienic and aesthetic problems posed by Melbourne's flourishing public street life. When you're done peering through the railings, calculate the number of cafés in the city, multiply it by the capacity of the human bladder, compare it with the number of current *pissoirs*, and pronounce Melbourne an absurd town. Recently listed by the National Trust as 'being of national significance', it squats on the corner of Russell and Bourke Streets. Nearby is 'A History Apparatus', a contemporary public sculpture by Chris Reynold that's sure to bemuse.

City North

National Museum of Victoria

The National Museum was founded in 1854 and is housed in the same building as the State Library. Over half a million people visit the museum each year, puffing and panting through excellent dioramas of Australian fauna, collections of minerals, rocks and fossils, plus a famous exhibit of Phar Lap, the world-renowned Australian race horse. The museum also has a planetarium, a children's museum, and an extensive range of Aboriginal artefacts. Visitors are encouraged to learn more about Koori culture via guided tours ($2) which are available each Thursday from 10am.

The museum, which is soon to close for major modification, is open daily 10am-5pm. Admission is $5.30 ($2.60 for children and concession card holders).

State Library

Australia's first state library was opened in 1854 and the concrete dome over the majestic Queen's Reading room added in 1908 (at the time it was the largest of its kind in the world). Surrounded by tree-filled lawns and assorted statuary, the library was initially conceived by Melbourne's civic elders as a world-class resource where all and sundry could gain access to education and the arts. Their philanthropy has since resulted in a mind-boggling collection of books (over one million would you believe!), periodicals, maps, manuscripts, paintings and photographs that would excite the most discerning philologist. A good time to visit and experience the rarefied atmosphere inside is a Sunday afternoon while outside soap-box orators, teens on skateboards, and activists loud-mouthing Premier Kennett, congregate in the library's forecourt.

The State Library is on the corner of Swanston and La Trobe Streets, and is open daily.

Royal Melbourne Institute of Technology (RMIT)

A block north of the State Library and National Museum is the head-turning facade of the RMIT. The award-winning though daffy design - the architect was presumably following the principles of chaos theory, or was on drugs - is a gem-like maze of green and purple patterns which look like they've been dropped and put back together, and a cavernous entrance that has been likened to a 'painfully stretched sphincter'. Initially deemed a failure, the new design has since won over Melburnians who now regard consistency as inexcusably boring. Check out the luminescent interior with its panels of light fittings, auditoriums, lecture theatres, galleries, and gleaming floors cleaned with a determined sense of hygiene. Astonishing!

Old Melbourne Gaol

Undoubtedly Melbourne's most viscerally disturbing site, the Old Melbourne Gaol houses a grisly yet fascinating collection of material from 19th century prison life. The gaol, built between 1841-64 and originally based on the Model Prison at Pentonville, England, was used to accommodate both short-term prisoners as well as some of the colony' most notorious criminals such as the bushranger Ned Kelly who was hanged here along with 134 others (the first were two Tasmanian Aborigines in 1842) before its closure in 1929. During World War II the compound was briefly re-opened as a military detention barracks and is now a museum where visitors can shudder through rooms and corridors filled with macabre death masks, lashing triangles, cat-o'-nine-tails, armour and the scaffold on which Ned Kelly dropped from sight forever. (Apparently his last words before dropping from the scene were 'Such is life'.)

The museum is on Russell Street and is open daily 9.30am-4.30pm. Admission is $6.50 (concessions are available). Guided tours can also be taken every Wednesday and Sunday night from 8.45pm and cost $15 for adults and $8 for children.

Royal Exhibition Building
Built in 1879, the Royal Exhibition Building gained international recognition when it was first used as a venue for the Great Exhibition of 1880. Australia's largest building at the time then became the seat of the first Federal Parliament in 1901. Exhibitions of homewares, computers and the like still take place in the building while the surrounding gardens - all elms and oaks and a fountain that glows green at night - are a lovely place for summer strolls.

The Royal Exhibition Building is immediately north of the city centre between Rathdowne and Nicholson streets.

City South
Southgate
One of Melbourne's shining new developments is just south of the city centre facing Flinders Street Station. Rising brashly from its riverside location and surrounded by a clutter of lesser buildings jostling for attention, the complex is jam-packed with smart-set cafés, bars and restaurants, foodhalls, shops and boutiques, a hotel plus a reasonably interesting aquarium that is tethered from the roof. Alongside is the Crown Casino complex stretching almost half a kilometre with more of the same but on a larger scale.

Victorian Arts Centre
Opened in 1982, the Victorian Arts Centre with its distinctive 115-metre steel spire (at night watch as

seagulls circle upwards into the light pursuing insects) is Melbourne's foremost cultural resource. The complex encompasses the Melbourne Concert Hall (a major venue for performing arts), the Performing Arts Museum (which showcases the world of popular entertainment and includes the Barry Humphries, Split Enz and Skyhooks costume collections), three major theatres plus several restaurants. It is also the home of the Australian Ballet, Australian Opera and the Victorian State Opera, as well as the Melbourne Theatre Company.

Guided tours through the sumptuous interiors are available Monday to Saturday, with a backstage tour on Sunday. The Victorian Arts Centre is on St Kilda Road immediately south of the Yarra River and city centre, and is open from 9am until late.

National Gallery of Victoria

The National Gallery was established in 1861 and has the largest and most encyclopaedic collection of art in Australia. The imposing bluestone building, designed by the late Sir Roy Grounds, holds a trove of artistic treasure from antiquity to the present day including the fruits of Titian, Rembrandt, Picasso, Turner, Auguste Rodin and Henry Moore. There are also magnificent rooms filled with Aboriginal, Asian, and contemporary art, important Australian paintings such as Tom Roberts *Shearing the Rams* and Frederick McCubbins *The Pioneer*, and exhibits of sculpture, photography, ceramics, costumes and textiles. A must see is the Great Hall which has a magnificent stained glass ceiling reputed to be the largest in the world. The gallery's only drawbacks are a stuffy atmosphere, poor visitor amenities and a general lack of exhibition space but a $160 million refurbishment should redress these problems. However the National Gallery of Victoria's planned upgrade, beginning in late 1998, means its closure for three years. A temporary site to display the art collection has, at the time of writing, yet to be named.

The National Gallery adjoins the Victorian Arts Centre at 180 St Kilda Road, and is open daily 10am-5pm. Admission is free.

City West

Rialto Towers

This twin tower of the vertiginous and vainglorious stands 242m high, and is the tallest building in the Southern Hemisphere (it is also the 47th tallest structure in the world). Take the high-speed lift to the 55th floor Observation Deck for 360-degree panoramic views of railyards, docks, bridges, parking buildings and Melbourne's never-ending suburbia. Powerful in-house binoculars ensure a better view while a handily placed café offers visitors some respite from the 'antartic' winds. There's also an audio visual display, a tiny museum documenting the city's history, a tourist shop selling everything from koala ties to lurid day-glo jumpers, and plenty of interactive live-action cameras. Broad city vistas don't come cheap - admission is $6 (perhaps the reason many choose this site as the place to make a marriage proposal). Find the Rialto Towers at 525 Collins Street, where its open daily 11am-11.30pm. Last one to the top is a rotten egg...

Melbourne Exhibition Centre

Melbourne's latest $130 million landmark is the largest exhibition centre in Australia as well as one of the most modern and best equipped complexes in the world. Its striking roof - which sweeps up in a giant curve not unlike Premier Kennetts brilliantined quiff - measures some 350m long and over 80m wide. The complex also has over 90,000 sq metres of exhibition space. Described not unflatteringly as a 'shed with spirit', it boasts an enormous glass-walled concourse, moveable walls, auditoriums, business and meeting rooms, lobbies, and parking for almost 2000 vehicles.

The DCM-designed Melbourne Exhibition Centre was awarded the 1996 building of the year by the Royal Australian Institute of Architects (RAIA). It is next to the Spencer Street bridge opposite the World Congress Centre.

Polly Woodside Maritime Museum

The focal point of this nautical museum is the restored

barque *Polly Woodside*, built in Belfast in 1885 and now moored in the historic Dukes and Orrs Dry Dock. Visitors can experience a sailing ship similar to those that founded and shaped Australia, or catch a ride on the recently rebuilt $1.5 million *Enterprize*, a replica of the schooner which brought the first settlers to Melbourne from Tasmania (the new model is equipped with modern luxuries such as toilets, computers and faxes, and began carrying passengers early in 1997). The museum also has displays of the city's maritime heritage, plus there's souvenir stores, a lighthouse and enough activities to satiate any childs hyperactive soul.

The *Polly Woodside* and museum are next door to the Melbourne Exhibition Centre, and open daily from 10am-4pm. Admission is $7 for adults and $4 for children.

City East
Old Treasury Building
Constructed in 1858 and designed by a gifted 19-year old draftsman named JJ Clark, this classical building with its elegant Doric columns and iron lamps is regarded as one of the most sophisticated structures in Australia. Once a repository for vast deposits of gold, it now houses a splendid exhibition tracing the city's past and present social and architectural history. Recently restored, the building is on Spring Street opposite the Treasury Gardens, and open daily 9am-5pm.

Parliament House
Melbourne's most imperious building ranks as one of the finest achievements of Victorian architecture in the world. Begun in 1852 and completed around 1892, its interiors - modelled on London's House of Lords and House of Commons and including a magnificent Corinthian-style parliamentary chamber - are where Australia's first Federal Government sat from 1901 before moving to Canberra in 1927. The exterior is dominated by massive Doric columns and Italianate balustrades, while sweeping front steps lead down to the top of Bourke Street.

Tours are available when parliament is not in session (March-May and September-November) every Monday to

Friday at 10 and 11am, noon, and 2, 3, and 3.45pm. At the rear is a picturesque landscape garden enclosed by fencing which is also open to the public.

Parliament House has recently been earmarked for an $80 million expansion.

Melbourne Cricket Ground (MCG)

The MCG, a 10-minute stroll east of the city centre, is a national sporting icon capable of holding up to 100,000 spectators. Originally created in 1853 as a simple cricket pitch, the ground was considerably transformed in 1956 when Melbourne hosted the Olympic Games. It is now the country's principal venue for watching Australian Football League (AFL) and international cricket matches, as well as playing host to a memorable range of concerts and events. (It often seems that if the MCG didn't exist, neither would Melbourne.)

A wander backstage will reveal pictorial walkways, staircases, crannies, halls too narrow to swing a cat, and stately museums and exhibitions. Most important is the Australian Gallery of Sport and Olympic Museum at the front of the members entrance. This three-tiered complex houses enough sporting memorabilia - from football and cricket to rowing and yachting - to induce dementia, and includes hands-on exhibits plus a permanent collection of past and present Olympic history.

It is open daily 10am-4pm with tours held hourly 10am-3pm. Admission is $6 for adults and $3 for children. For more tour details contact the MCG on 9657 8879.

Gardens

Royal Botanic Gardens

The much-visited Royal Botanic Gardens, between Alexandra and Birdwood Avenues in South Yarra, are rightly regarded as one of the finest examples of landscape gardening in the world. The 100-acre expanse, enclosed by a perennial border of perfumed flowers and shrubbery, was established in 1846 and is renowned for its rolling parks and lawns that hold over 110,000 individual plants from around the world. The gardens also abound with native fauna such as rabbits, possums and fruit bats as well as a variety of birdlife. After strolling along the shaded pathways - some specked with sunlight filtering through the trees - you can stop off at the lakeside tearoom (which serves expensive Devonshire teas and snacks) or potter through one of the many garden specialty shops.

Visitors can pick up a map at the main gate which lists the gardens attractions, while free guided tours leave the Visitor Centre from Tuesday to Friday and Sunday at 10am and 11am. There's also a 'twilight' guided tour most days when birds and plants are more noticeable (this should be booked in advance at the Visitor Centre) and an interactive botanic audio tour claimed to be the world's first. The gardens, which also host open-air theatre performances, deck-chair musical concerts and movie screenings during summer, are open daily 7.30am-5pm. Entry is free.

King's Domain

Spreading north and west of the Royal Botanic Gardens is the King's Domain, an informal parkland endowed with gardens, rockeries and waterfalls. Dominating the south-west corner of the park is the enormous *Shrine of Remembrance*, built from 1927-34 to commemorate the men and women who served during World War I and World War II. One of its many features is the *Rock of Remembrance*, the centre of which is illuminated by a ray of sunlight at the 11th hour of the 11th day of the 11th month on Armistice Day. The annual Anzac Day ceremony is held here on April 25 (the date that the Australian and New Zealand combined forces landed at Gallipoli during World War I) with a dawn service followed by a procession along St Kilda Road into the city. The shrine is open daily 10am-5pm.

Immediately east is *La Trobes Cottage*, home of the states first Lieutenant Governor, Charles Joseph La Trobe. The pre-fabricated cottage was built in England then transported to Australia in 1839, and is open Saturday to Thursday 10am-4pm. Admission is $4.

Among the domain's other attractions are an observatory, herbarium and the *Queen Victoria Gardens* to the north. The latter is where you'll find the well-known

Floral Clock as well as a frumpy statue of Queen Victoria with the figures of Progress, History, Wisdom and Justice surrounding the base.

King's Domain is south-east of the city centre, and bordered by St Kilda Road, Domain Road, Anderson Street and the Yarra River.

Fitzroy and Treasury Gardens

Dividing the parliamentary precinct from East Melbourne, the Fitzroy Gardens were originally a rat-infested refuse tip but are today one of the most attractive landscaped city parks in Melbourne. The gardens, designed in 1857 and originally laid out in a formal Union Jack pattern, hold a popular herbarium, where chattering brides marry in a frenzy of camera flashes, and *Captain Cooks Cottage* which was shipped to the country from England and rebuilt here to mark Melbourne's centenary in 1934. The great explorer's parental home, with its stone and creeper-covered walls, contains a number of 18th-century period furnishings and is surrounded by a well-appointed garden. The cottage attracts over 300,000 visitors annually, and is open daily 9am-5pm. Admission is $2.50. Security has recently been beefed up after a chest reputedly owned by Cook was stolen (it was returned soon after).

Adjacent to the Fitzroy Gardens are the Treasury Gardens. Created in 1867, the gardens contain Moreton Bay Fig trees, small fountains and pools, and a memorial to US President John F Kennedy. Protesters often congregate here before marching to Parliament.

Flagstaff Gardens

The Flagstaff Gardens are just south of the Queen Victoria Markets. The enclosure was originally an Aboriginal burial site (local Aborigines also used the spot as a lookout where they first observed Melbournes earliest pioneers sailing up Port Phillip Bay), later becoming a resting place for white settlers then a signalling station in 1840 announcing the arrival of incoming vessels. Gardens were added in the 1860s and its now an Eden of elm and oak trees, shrubbery and flowers that detonate into colour during season. At lunchtime during weekdays the Flagstaff Gardens are often crowded with city workers having lunch or playing sport (little has changed since post-industrialisation when city parks were built to improve both the quality of life and the productivity of the workers).

Suburbs

Fitzroy

The suburb of Fitzroy is just north-east of the city centre. For many years it has attracted a general drift of bored suburbanites, comedians and hippy-dips in search of a little *frisson*. The focal point remains Brunswick Street, a lively strip of cafés and restaurants, exotic bazaars and second-hand furniture shops. Every possible kind of person is on promenade here: men and women in gym gear with Coppertone skins; crystal gazers with rings and studs pushed through eyebrows, nostrils, ear lobes, lips and belly buttons; black-clad arty types and *louche* bohemians drinking little cups of coffee; and shopkeepers shaking Afghan rugs and muttering through whiskers.

Other popular thoroughfares include Johnston Street, the home of Melbourne's Spanish population and the best place to go for tapas, and Smith Street, the Fitzroy border abutting Collingwood. Here you'll find health food stores, Asian groceries and a range of custom-made goods.

To get to Fitzroy from the city centre, take Tram Nos 9, 10 or 11 east along Collins Street for Brunswick Street, and Tram Nos 86, 88 or 89 for Smith Street.

Carlton

The charming enclave of Carlton, immediately west of Fitzroy, is Melbourne's centre of Italian culture and cuisine. Liberally sprinkled with restaurants, bistros, delis and food stores perfect for stocking up on authentic victuals, the suburb is also home to some of the city's finest examples of Victorian architecture as well as its general cemetery.

Lygon Street is where most begin a visit to the suburb. Although subject to recent modernisation, this pastel-shaded, neon-lit strip remains a fine place for noodling among specialty shops and boutiques, settling back at one of the many cafés or gelatarias - overflowing with lotharios and dolled-up women - and admiring the streams of late-model cars vying for parking space.

To get there, take Tram Nos 1, 15, 21 or 22 from Swanston Street for Lygon Street. Buses from Russell Street and Flinders Street Station also traverse Carlton.

Parkville

A short walk west of Lygon Street is the historic Melbourne University. First begun in 1854 (lectures followed a year later), its terrific old buildings, landscape gardens (open daily), and sculptures and murals provide an ideal setting for a large range of cultural events including film, theatre, music, dance, visual arts and, of course, lectures. There's also the Ian Potter Gallery showcasing exhibitions of contemporary art, and a museum dedicated to Percy Grainger, a rather quaint composer who loved roaming the world and goofing off to folk music. The latter is open Monday to Friday 10am-4pm. You can find it near Gate 8 on Royal Parade.

Another of Parkville's major attractions is the *Royal Melbourne Zoological Gardens*. Established in 1857, it is the oldest operating zoo in Australia as well as the third oldest in the world. It is also one of the most attractive, combining Victorian landscaped gardens with hi-tech enclosures (some employing horticultural tricks to create the illusion animals are in their natural habitat) holding over 350 species of native Australian and exotic animals from around the world. Highlights include the steamy Butterfly House (where hundreds of Australian butterflies alight upon visitors), the African rainforest (filled with lions, leopards and pygmy hippopotamus), the World of Frogs, and seal feeding time. The zoos focus on furthering environmental education has led to a number of research and conservation programs, as well as the breeding of rare and endangered species such as Sumatran tigers and snow leopards.

The zoo is open daily 9am-5pm. Admission is $12 for adults, $6 for children and $33 for families. To get there, take Tram Nos 18, 19 or 20 from Elizabeth Street along Royal Parade to Stop 16 where its a short walk to the zoo, or catch a train from Flinders Street Station on the Upfield or Gowrie lines. These run Monday through Saturday, and stop at Royal Park Station just outside the zoo gates.

Richmond

This suburb, east of the city centre, was in bygone times an area of narrow unmade roads, tiny cottages, and tanneries, abattoirs and wool-scouring works hugging the banks of the Yarra River. Today it is home to Melbourne's thriving Greek and Vietnamese communities (the former reputedly make up the third largest Greek population of any city in the world after Athens and Salonika) and streets lined with restaurants serving everything from taramasalata and pickled octopus to spicy *pho* (soup) and barbecued duck.

Richmond's main thoroughfares are Church Street, Swan Street, Victoria Street and Bridge Road. Apart from myriad cafés, restaurants and colourful old pubs, you can find cut-price designer stores, retro shops, and some of Melbourne's most fanciful landmarks including the *Dimmeys* department store, 140 Swan Street, filled with dishevelled displays of junk and knick-knackery at bargain-basement prices.

To get to Richmond, take Tram Nos 48, 75 or 76 for Bridge Road, Tram No 70 tram for Swan Street, and Tram Nos 44 or 45 for Victoria Street. Tram Nos 23, 24 and 42 also run to west Richmond while trains journey to both west and east Richmond.

South Yarra and Toorak

Both suburbs, to the south of the Yarra River, are the favourites of Melbourne's wealthy scions and the shop-til-you-drop set. During balmy summer days, their main streets are cram-full with more money, more champagne, more cellphones and more cleavage than almost anywhere else in Australia. Apart from posturing hotels and boutiques, they also have the kind of restaurants - wall-to-wall with regulation hardwood plinths, white linen tables and deliriously loud music - the plain and thrifty studiously try to avoid.

The two distinctive faces of these suburbs are Toorak Road and Chapel Street. Toorak Road proliferates in

Mercedes Benz drivers, sensibly dressed men gathering mobile phones, and coiffed women in fulgent furs walking poodles and bichon frises (most poofily groomed and done up in little caps and jackets to complement their owners). Chapel Street is a far more funkier domain (it wouldn't be hard) with the fortyish real-estate agents and their wives making way for the young and nimble figured. Fashion and attitude count here. So does eating out. But, according to Melbourne's best-known and most astute culinary critic Stephen Downes, even though restaurants may be full, that doesn't always mean the quality of the food or service is high.

Together South Yarra and Toorak can only muster a modicum of sights. The stand-out among a sea of schmalzy cream-coloured buildings (most done up in mock French Provincial style) is undoubtedly *Como House*, a colonial mansion built in 1847 by Edward Williams who was aided by the noted garden designer William Sangster. Supposedly named after Lake Como in Italy, the mansion boasts impressive architecture (a mixture of Regency and Italianate styles) and five acres of sloping lawns, land- scape gardens, and pine and cypress glades. Currently owned by the National Trust, it's at 16 Como Avenue, and open daily 10am-5pm.

To get to South Yarra, take Tram No 8 or 72 from Swanston Street. Trains also leave from the Flinders Street Station on the Sandringham line to South Yarra Station.

St Kilda

One of Melbourne's most beguiling yet sophisticated suburbs, St Kilda is a place where you can talk, eat, protest, browse or simply hang out. Originally named after the British schooner *The Lady of St Kilda*, which was often seen sailing on Port Phillip Bay in the 1840s, the former seaside resort has played host to both the rich and poor over the years.

In the boom era of the 1880s, Melbournes wealthy began building large homes in the area. Buoyed by this new influx, St Kilda soon prospered, becoming a fashionable and popular place to live. But by the 1960s, St Kildas fortunes had dramatically waned. Its once lavish residences were either demolished or converted in to cheap flats and rooming homes, and Fitzroy Street, formerly among the city's more illustrious boulevards, became the haunt of prostitutes and drug dealers.

Today St Kilda is an intricate mix of modern din and bustle and yesteryear allure. Its main streets are lined with second-hand furniture and Art Deco stores, bookshops, and café latte emporiums while its human potpourri - from raisin-eyed fundamentalists raving about salvation to activists clutching clipboards - only add to the suburbs diverse appeal.

A tailor-made way to experience St Kilda's rich history is by heritage walking. The *St Kilda Heritage Walk* brochure (free from the St Kilda Town Hall, cnr St Kilda Road and Carlisle Street) nicely captures 22 historical points of interest including *Alfred Square*, the first building erected in the area (around 1840), the Spanish Mission -style *Belvedere*, and the *St Kilda Botanical Gardens* (1859) which have evergreen enclosures, a conservatory, a duck pond, rose gardens and a good children's playground.

Another attraction on St Kilda's long list of things to see is *Luna Park*. Established in 1912, this fun park with its distinctive laughing face has a mix of mostly sedate rides like the ferris wheel, ghost train and a carousel that's all pink-cheeked cherubs and gaily painted horses. Entry is free with half-day tickets (which include unlimited rides) priced at $14 and family tickets at $37. Concessions are also available. Restoration work has slowly begun on some of the park's attractions with the current garish colours being returned to their original colour scheme. Luna Park is only open weekends and public holidays.

Visitors should also check out the *Esplanade*, a 10km stretch of track shared by cyclists, roller bladers and walkers, and take the kiddies for a ride on the Shetland ponies along the foreshore, or promenade on the *St Kilda Pier*. This is at its best on a hot summer night, when people, sucking icy-poles and smelling of chips, pace up and down the walkway awaiting the 'southerly buster'.

The two thoroughfares dominating St Kilda are the brash Fitzroy Street with its takeaway shops, restaurants and stylish neon-lit bars, and the Jewish heartland of

Acland Street. Here you'll find even more cafés and restaurants plus cake shops, delicatessens and designer clothes and homeware stores.

To get to St Kilda, take Tram No 96 west along Bourke Street, Tram Nos 15 or 16 south along Swanston Street or Nos 10, 11 or 12 west along Collins Street. Bus No 246 from Russell Street also travels to St Kilda.

Williamstown

Williamstown lies at the mouth of the Yarra River about a 10-minute drive south-west of the city centre over the Westgate bridge. Formerly Melbourne's major seaport, Williamstown has retained a maritime village atmosphere with its picturesque foreshore, closely stood terrace houses heavily adorned with iron lace, and enticing tree-lined streets.

Williamstown is a fine place for serendipitous exploring, especially through the older parts of the town. This is where you'll find some of Melbourne's finest historical buildings such as the areas around *Nelson Place* (named after the triumphal British Admiral Horatio Nelson who whupped the French and Spanish in the Battle of Trafalgar) and the *Historical Society Museum* at 5 Electra Place. Originally constructed in 1860, this excellent repository of seafaring history has period furniture and an abundance of model ships. Its open every Sunday 2-5pm, and admission is $2 for adults (children free).

Other favourite pastimes are a visit to *Fort Gellibrand*, mooring spot for convict ships in the 1840s, and the *Williamstown Railway Museum* which features a fine collection of steam locomotives, wagons and old carriages. The latter is open every weekend noon-5pm, and admission is $4 for adults and $2 for children.

There are also characterful pubs, a slew of art galleries and handicraft stores plus *Siren*, one of the city's best restaurants located at the Beach Pavilion (see the *Eating Out* chapter). If you want to avoid the crowds, plan a visit outside weekends, when the community is overrun with city-based sightseers and pert, well-scrubbed tourists.

Williamstown can be reached by both land and sea. To get there, take a weekend tram to St Kilda Pier (Stop 32) and then catch a ferry to Williamstown. Trains also depart regularly from Flinders Street and Spencer Street Stations, while a *City Wanderer* bus travels to Williamstown from Flinders Street.

Other Attractions

Ripponlea

This historic site is one of Melbourne's most enduring legacies of the 19th century 'Marvellous Melbourne era'. Built and owned by Sir Frederick Sargood, a noted businessman and politician who made his fortune selling material during the goldrush boom, it features a 33-room brick mansion, a Hollywood-style swimming pool, and over five hectares of gardens enclosing sculptured gardens and lawns, trees and fernery, as well as an ornamental lake, grottoes, boathouse, and a conservatory.

The estate, which has proved a popular picnic spot for Melburnians, is currently undergoing a $5 million facelift by the National Trust who hope to restore Ripponlea as Australia's foremost historic house. Work is already underway with the reinstatement of a wrought-iron perimeter fence which will be followed by the introduction of new carpets and the restoration of the conservatory.

Ripponlea is at 192 Hotham Street in the suburb of Elsternwick, south of the city centre. Its open Tuesday to Sunday 10am-5pm, and admission is $5 for adults, $4 for children and $18.50 for families.

Museum of Modern Art (Heide)

The Museum of Modern Art was founded by Sunday and John Reed who encouraged some of Australia's greatest artistic talent including Sidney Nolan (who was born in Melbourne in 1917), Arthur Boyd, Albert Tucker, John Perceval and Joy Hester. Set in a glorious expanse of natural bush and parkland, the museum encompasses changing exhibitions of local and international 20th -century art, and boasts an impressive sculpture park, kitchen garden and courtyard, as well as the prize-winning home of the Reeds. There is also a smart restaurant at the museum's entrance for those who don't pack a picnic.

The museum, originally the home of the Heidelberg School (named after Melbourne's sylvan suburb where many of Australia's leading Impressionists first painted) and the Angry Penguins, is at 7 Templestowe Road in Bullen, about 15 minutes drive from the city centre. Its open Tuesday to Friday 10am-5pm, and on weekends and public holidays noon-5pm. Admission is $5 for adults with children free.

Scienceworks Museum

Opened in 1992 on the former site of an old pumping station, Scienceworks is an eight-hectare complex combining science and technology in a variety of 'hands on' exhibits (some of which are quite bizarre). All those things you always wanted to know but were too afraid to ask - how are cars built? what is energy? can I build a nuclear reactor out of compost? - will be answered with practised aplomb. The museum also has a frenzied barbecue area and playground, plus there's live theatre and spectacular educational shows on the earth's history. Visitors should remember, however, that many of the displays are not recommended for people with heart conditions and hearing impairments because of sudden loud noises.

Scienceworks Museum is at 2 Booker Street in Spotswood, about 5km from the city centre. Its open daily 10am-4.30pm, and admission is $10 for adults and $5 for children (concessions are available).

Day Trips Around Melbourne

The regions around Melbourne provide a popular day-trip destination for Melburnians and Melbourne-based visitors alike. Among the many attractions are spectacular beaches, elegant historical towns, popular spa resorts, verdant woodlands ideal for hiking, lush wine-producing areas, wildlife sanctuaries and artist's colonies.

Most of the following sights are easily reached by public transport or by car.

Geelong

Geelong lies on Corio Bay about a one-hour drive south of Melbourne. The area was originally used as grazing pasturage by Melbourne's earliest pioneers and has since grown to become the state's largest provincial city (population 180,000) as well as an important industrial centre and port.

Although the majority of visitors use Geelong as a gateway to the Great Ocean Road, it does offer enough attractions to make a stop worthwhile. Foremost among these is the *National Wool Centre*, on the corner of Brougham and Moorabool streets. Housed in a refurbished bluestone woolstore, the complex has an excellent museum tracing the history of wool in Australia from early settlement to the present day, as well as handicraft and clothing shops, and a café. Its open daily 10am-5pm.

Geelong's other sights include the *Geelong Art Gallery* (admission $3) showcasing both colonial and contemporary Australian art, and the lovely Art Deco promenade *sea baths*, while walks in almost any direction will lead you to over 200 National Trust-registered buildings. The city has recently received a massive injection of government funds which will be used to upgrade the waterfront and its tourist facilities.

En route to Geelong is **Werribee**, site of a number of historic homesteads such as *Werribee Park mansion*. Built in the 1880s and hemmed in by 10 hectares of formal gardens featuring fountains, lakes and grottoes, this fabulously restored Italianate building has antiques and furnishings illustrating the splendour of 19th-century wealth. (On a hot summers day you can sit back and imagine businessmen in frockcoats and top hats escorting their ladies, parasol in hand, up the garden path so to speak.) Adjacent to Werribee Park is a reasonably good zoo which has safari rides to better see the African and Australian animals in the grounds.

Bellarine Peninsula

This peninsula, just east of Geelong, is one of Melbourne's most popular and fashionable holiday destinations. An increasingly growing number of visitors flock here for the surfing beaches, excellent fishing and diving spots, and seaside resorts including the once-exclusive **Queenscliff**. Here you'll find grandiose hotels (some with a noticeable European ambience), well-appointed guesthouses and old-world cafés serving everything from beer-battered harpuka to kangaroo sausage. Lodgings and food aside, Queenscliff also summons up enough sights and activities to make a stopover compulsory.

Queenscliff is 90 minutes drive from Melbourne. An alternative means of getting there is to catch the car ferry shuttling every two hours during the day from Sorrento.

Ballarat

Victoria's largest inland city (population 90,000) is around 110km west of Melbourne. Born from the gold-mining period between 1851-61, Ballarat is today a place of wide tree-lined avenues, showpiece parks and gardens, galleries and museums, and grand Victorian buildings.

The city's premier attraction is the not-to-be-missed *Sovereign Hill*, an award-winning tourist township that recreates the mining shafts, tents, hotels, schools, shops and mullock heaps of the goldrush. Visitors can pan for gold in a nearby stream or simply observe the working and living conditions that existed last century. Sovereign Hill also holds twice-nightly sound and light shows - dramatically called 'Blood on the Southern Cross' - each day on the Eureka Stockade (Australia's only armed insurrection which took place in 1854 at Ballarat). The township is south of the city centre, and open daily 9.30am-5pm. Admission is $16.50 for adults, $8.50 for children, and $44 for families. Tickets for the show are $19.50 for adults, $9.50 for children, and $52 for families.

More great things to see in and around Ballarat include the *Gold Museum* (displaying an aureate array of nuggets, coins and alluvial gold), the *Robert Clarke Horticultural Centre* (a stupendous structure that looks like a fallen crystal rather than a simple glasshouse attraction filled with flowers and shrubbery), the recently opened *Great Southern Woolshed* (a huge corrugated iron shed revealing Australia's rich heritage of wool production), and the Gothic-style *Kryal Castle* (reputedly the third-largest castle in the world). Theres also a number of fine art galleries, a popular wildlife and reptile park, botanic gardens perfect for picnics, and a number of bucolic B&Bs if you fancy staying over for the night.

Daylesford and Hepburn Springs

Daylesford and Hepburn Springs are a two-hour drive north-west of Melbourne. Known as Victorias spa centre, these twin towns combine to provide world-beating mineral springs, excellent rural cuisine, and a bank of attractions and activities.

Visitors to Daylesford usually make a beeline to the tastefully restored *Convent Gallery*, a former nunnery and now a commercial gallery attracting over 4000 people a week. Cradled in pleasant gardens, the building includes two floors of mostly mediocre artworks and a slightly better café. The Convent Gallery is on Daly Street and is open daily 10am-6pm. Admission is $3. A short stroll away are the historic *Botanic Gardens* (laid out in 1863) and, to the south-west, lovely *Lake Daylesford* where spots can be picnicked, boats hired, and tracks walked.

The appealing *spa complex* at Hepburn Springs is one of the world's biggest and most popular spots to 'take the waters', and is frequently booked up months ahead with Australian and overseas tourists. It's also home to the country's largest massage centre where over 40 masseurs work tirelessly patting and pummelling bodies back into shape. As well as spa baths and massages, the resort offers a variety of treatments such as body wraps and flotation tank therapies. Its open weekdays 10am-8pm, and weekends 9am-8pm.

Bendigo

Bendigo (population 67,000) is another gold-mining site of the 1850s. Just under two-hours drive north-west of Melbourne, this thriving provincial city retains imposing traces of Victorian architecture - including the post office, hotels and private residences - redolent of a once prosperous age plus mines, good art and science centres, as well as a range of outdoor pursuits.

Among Bendigo's attractions is the popular *Central Deborah Mine*. Guided tours ($12 for adults, $6 for children) allow visitors to don hard hats and miners lights and travel over 60 metres underground to experience how gold was once unearthed. The mine is on Violet Street, south of Rosalind Park, and open daily 9am-5pm. From here you can take a tour on a Talking Tram - an authentically restored tramcar offering a commentary on Bendigo's history and architecture - to the city centre.

North of the city centre is the *Joss House*, a Chinese place of worship and one of Bendigo's original buildings. Classified by the National Trust, it features a good collection of ornamental paintings and memorials to the dead. Also worth investigating are the excellent Bendigo Art Gallery, the 'hands-on' Discovery Science and Technology Centre, plus several ceramic and craft stores.

For outdoor enthusiasts there's bushwalking at the nearby Bendigo Creel Linear Park, and fishing, boating and swimming at Lake Eppalock, south east of the city.

Montsalvat

In 1934 Justus Jorgensen bought a tract of bushland with the intention of establishing a unique artists colony. Montsalvat became exactly that and today remains an important venue for hosting visual arts, studies, performances and exhibitions. The colony - reminiscent of a simple French provincial village - attracts artists, buyers and visitors worldwide while its clutch of mud and timber-walled buildings regularly host wedding parties as well as the Montsalvat National Poets Festival. Sadly, the annual Montsalvat International Jazz Festival has been axed. In July 1996 a fire almost raised a heritage-listed barn, in the process destroying precious artworks. Montsalvat has stayed open, however, and is 26km north-east of the city in Hillcrest Avenue, Eltham, ph 9439 87761. You can see it daily 9am-5pm, and admission is $5.

Yarra Valley

The Yarra Valley, 80 minutes east of Melbourne via the Maroondah Highway, has some of the most beautiful countryside in the state - a patchwork of historic vineyards, brunet furrows of rich farmland, and Millet-like stacks of hay. It also has a diverse range of walking trails, great opportunities for nature watching as well as activities such as fishing, kayaking, hot-air ballooning and picnicking.

The areas most popular tourist attraction is the *Healesville Sanctuary* on Badger Creek Road. Opened in 1934 and located in natural bushland, the complex includes a curvilinear building described as a 'platypa-morphic' piece of architecture, and walk-through enclosures containing a large variety of native Australian animals (wombats, koalas, echidnas, platypus, kangaroos, emus, eagles and other fauna overseas visitors can't get enough of). Visitors are introduced to exhibitions such as the nocturnal house through a series of spaces, each more dimly lit than the preceding so eyes can adjust to low lighting levels. The sanctuary is open daily 9am-5pm and admission is $12. Nearby is Badger Creek, an idyllic setting ideal for picnics and barbecues.

Good sightseeing and nature walks through ancient sassafras trees, mountain ash - the world's tallest hardwood trees - and abandoned camps and sawmills can be found in the *Kingslake National Park* and the newly opened *Yarra Ranges National Park*, while eco-adventure tours are available at Mystic Mountains, an area of towering eucalyptus and fern trees.

Cork-sniffers can also visit over 30 wineries including Domaine Chandon, a sparkling wine producer established by French giant Moet et Chandon in 1986. Its open daily 10.30am-4.30pm. Others are open daily or on weekends, and offer cellar door sales and the opportunity to taste exquisite, hand-crafted wines. The Yarra Valley also has excellent cafés and bistros serving everything from venison to Devonshire teas, plus a range of antique and bric-a-brac shops (pioneer relics are everywhere).

The Dandenong Ranges

The Dandenong Ranges ('Dandenong' is derived from the Aboriginal word 'tanjenong', meaning 'lofty mountain') rise sluggishly over Melbournes eastern fringes. For over a century these ranges (hills more like!) have been a popular weekend destination, and now attract over 3.5 million visitors a year. The area is endowed with towns and villages, teahouses serving Devonshire teas and gardens filled with tulips and rhododendrons, while bushwalks lead into some of the region's rural loveliness.

The Dandenongs focal point is *Puffing Billy*, Victoria's oldest surviving and most famously preserved steam locomotive winding through 13km of forest and fern gullies from Belgrave to Emerald Lake Park. The steam train runs daily except Christmas Day, and costs $15.50 for adults, and $9 for children (family concessions are available). Plans are underway to lengthen the track to 24km which will extend the current travelling time of just over two hours. Adjacent to the Puffing Billy Station is a steam museum featuring a number of early locomotives.

Other attractions include *Ricketts Sanctuary*, a collection of 200 Aboriginal-influenced clay sculptures superimposed onto rocks by the artist William Ricketts, the *'Skyhigh'* lookout with glorious views over Port Phillip Bay and the city, and national parks filled with rainforests (some the home of the celebrated lyrebird) and vectored by trails. The area is also dotted with wonderfully decorated cottages and quaint B&Bs, antique shops, and galleries selling ceramics and craftware.

Mornington Peninsula

The boot-shaped Mornington Peninsula, forming the eastern shore of Port Phillip Bay about 90km south of Melbourne, is a popular resort area of swimming and surfing beaches, wineries, white-picketed stud farms, and national parks.

The peninsulas two principal beachfront towns are *Sorrento* and *Portsea*. Sorrento is home to an average aquarium, some impressive architecture (best seen by horse-drawn cab) and tour operators offering visitors the chance to swim with dolphins off the coast. Neighbouring Portsea has even grander architecture, good lookouts, and a range of activities including boating, snorkelling, cycling and hang-gliding.

Covering most of the peninsulas tip is the *Point Nepean National Park*, a great spot for picnicking and walking a series of short but challenging trails, while the *Mornington Peninsula National Park* is one of Victorias most visited destinations. Also worthwhile are browsing the areas many markets and craft shops, and taking a chairlift to the top of *Arthurs Seat* (named after a Scottish mountain and the peninsulas highest land form) for sublime views of the Mornington Peninsula and Port Phillip Bay.

Phillip Island

Phillip Island is about an hour-and-a-half drive south of Melbourne. In early October the 500cc motocyle Australian Grand Prix is held here. Most visitors come for its multitude of scenery, great surf coming off Bass Strait, and the fantastically popular *Penguin Parade*.

The parade, occurring each evening at Summerland Beach during the nesting season, attracts over three million visitors a year. The stars of the event are fairy penguins - the world's smallest penguin - which emerge from the ocean then waddle niminy-piminy to their nesting spots (delighted onlookers gape at their progress from elevated boardwalks and stands). Although flash photography is not allowed, you can buy postcards and souvenirs at the Penguin Parade Visitor Centre or catch an excellent visual display. Its open daily from 10am, and admission is $7.50 for adults and $3.50 for children.

The island is also home to the Koala Conservation Centre (open daily from 10am), Australia's largest colony of fur seals at Seals Rocks just off the western tip, mutton bird colonies around Cape Woolamai, a wildlife park where animal contact is encouraged, and the main township of Cowes which features a lovely promenade as well as Australia's largest maze.

Phillip Island's varied topography also allows for a wide rage of outdoor pursuits such as bird-watching (there are over 250 species of birdlife on the island), bushwalks, cycling, horse-riding, and rock-climbing.

For more information about the islands myriad attractions visit the Phillip Island Information Centre in Newhaven, ph (059) 56 7447, and open daily 10am-5pm. The island's tourist facilities are currently being upgraded with provision for a seal-watching facility at The Nobbies.

Great Ocean Road

The Great Ocean Road is unquestionably Melbourne's most popular outlying attraction. It starts at Torquay (just south of Geelong) then snakes its way along 300km of glorious coastline - part of it known as 'Shipwreck Coast' because over 100 ships floundered here - to Warrnambool (a popular spot for whale-watching).

Built as part of a series of public work programs initiated by the government during the Depression, the road passes artificial attractions such as quiet seaside towns (Torquay, Anglesea and Lorne) and spectacular natural features including caramel-coloured cliffs, inviting surf bays, and national parks and eucalyptus forest. Perhaps its most famous attraction is *The Twelve Apostles*, in the *Port Campbell National Park*, which are striking limestone rock stacks rising from the Southern Ocean. Apart from scenery, the Great Ocean Road area also offers good opportunities for diving and fishing, surfing monster waves, nature watching, bushwalking, and hang-gliding.

(Facing) The enormous, much revered Shrine of Remembrance. (Overleaf) The restored barque *Polly Woodside* at Melbourne's historic Duke's and Orr's Dry Dock [Above].The MCG, centre of homage for the city's sports-mad fans [Below].

Tours

Melbourne has a number of tours ranging from 10-minute interludes to month-long excursions in the city and outlying regions. For more information on operators and destinations, visit any information centre or check out independent publications available from leading newsagents, cafés and pubs.

Bus Tours

Coach companies such as Melbourne Sightseeing, Australian Pacific, AAT Kings, and Pioneer Gray Line offer similar tours to popular destinations including Ballarat, Phillip Island, the Great Ocean Road, Healesville Sanctuary, and the Dandenongs.

For city-based tours (in double-decker buses no less) to premier attractions try the following:

City Explorer, ph 9563 9788 - sights include the Shrine of Remembrance, the Royal Melbourne Zoological Gardens, Scienceworks, Captain Cooks Cottage, Queen Victoria Market, the Shrine of Remembrance and the Victorian Arts Centre, $15 for adults and $8 for children (family concessions are available).

City Wanderer, ph 9563 9788 - tours to similar sights, $15 for adults, $8 for children (family concessions available).

SouthSide Wanderer, ph 9563 9788 - tours to Melbourne's historic homes, gardens and beaches as well as destinations in the city's southern suburbs, $15 for adults and $8 for children (family concessions available).

Backpackers Tours

Tours designed especially for backpackers include:

Autopia Tours, ph 9326 5536 - organises one to two-day tours to Phillip Island, the Great Ocean Road, the Grampians and viticultural regions, prices from $45-65.

Macs Backpacker Tours, ph 052 413 180 - one to three-day tours along the Great Ocean Road, Phillip Island and Grampians plus bushwalking opportunities, prices from $50-100.

The One Day Tour, ph 054 291 627 - visits Mount Macedon, Magnetic Hill and Hanging Rock, also includes horse-riding, koala spotting and stopping for billy tea and damper in the bush, $67.50.

Lets Go Bush, ph 9614 3313 - one to two-day tours along the Great Ocean Road, the Dandenongs and Healesville Sanctuary, prices from $60-85.

River, Ocean and Gondola Cruises

Melbourne River Cruises, ph 9614 1215 - organises one-hour downriver tours passing Southgate, historic Victoria Docks, Crown Casino and the Polly Woodside Maritime Museum plus upriver one-hour tours passing the Victoria Arts Centre, Royal Botanic Gardens, MCG, and inner-city suburbs such as Richmond and Toorak, there are also two-and-a-half-hour downriver and upriver tours combining the attractions of both, departures for the three tours are dependent on season, prices from $13 (adults) and $6.50 (children), tickets can be bought from the Blue Kiosk on Princes Bridge.

Southgate River Tours, ph 9818 6870 - offers half-hour and one-hour trips on a refurbished ferry to inner-city suburbs, prices from $17.50 (adults) and $8 (children).

Wattle Steam Tug, ph 9328 2739 - operates one-and-a-half-hour cruises from Station Pier (Port Melbourne) on Sunday and public holidays from February to June and October to December, prices from $10.

Penguin Water Cruises, ph 0I5 311 922 - multitude of one-hour cruises from St Kilda Pier to see a local penguin colony, prices from $15-20.

Venice on the Yarra, ph 0411 114 736 - lavish Venetian-style gondola cruises for two to four people along the Yarra River, includes champagne cruises and breakfast, lunch or dinner cruises, discounts available during winter, prices from $55 for a breakfast cruise.

Williamstown Bay and River Cruises, 9397 2255 - ferry operating weekends and public holidays from the World Trade Centre, Southgate & St Kilda Pier to Williamstown.

Food Tours

Queen Victoria Markets Foodies Dream Tour, ph 0658 9601 - in-depth guide through one of Melbourne's busiest and most colourful destinations, prices from $15.

Food, The West Side Story, ph 9689 1186 - group tours to Footscray Market, prices from $30.

Food Lovers Tour of Melbourne, ph 9899 9299 - expensive but a food-lovers delight, includes a two-course lunch, prices from $120.

Talkabout Tours Chocolate Indulgence Walk, ph 9654 7555 - mouth-watering search for the city's best chocolate and desserts, prices from $20.

Little Asia Spring Tours, ph 9652 0733 - discover the gastronomic delights of Victoria Street in inner-city Richmond, tours reveal the best way to identify, choose and prepare a variety of cheap and nutritious vegetables found in Asian groceries and markets, popular three-hour tours are $44 per person (cost includes lunch at one of the areas many Vietnamese restaurants).

Melbourne Wholesale Fruit and Vegetable Market Tour, ph 9620 2089 - an electronic 'train' carries up to 30 passengers through a 30-hectare complex (the largest of its kind in Victoria) located close to the city, includes visits to the fruit and vegetable markets and National Flower Centre, operates weekdays 5am-8am at $12 per person (price includes breakfast).

Other Tours

Harley Davidson Tours, ph 9557 9122 - offers everything from 10-minute joy rides on a Heritage Softtail Harley to five-day tours, good motorbike trips along the spectacular Great Ocean Road, Reefton Spur, Phillip Island, Dandenong Ranges and around Port Phillip Bay, experienced guides plus interpreters available, price includes protective riding gear and insurance.

Day Tours by Bicycle, ph 9886 0800 - a range of leisurely paced, half-day guided bicycle tours that have both a cultural and scenic flavour, helmets and jackets provided.

Hang in There Adventure Sports, ph 1300 5533 663 - wilderness pursuits such as Nordic skiing, spelunking, abseiling, rock climbing, bushwalking and white-water rafting at a minimal cost, experienced guides always on hand, offers day trips to 12-day excursions.

Dreamtime Outback Safaris, ph 008 646 871 - specialist operator organising four-wheel drive (4WD) tours from three to five days, focus on Aboriginal culture (especially the exploration of Aboriginal lands), chartered safaris of up to one month available for groups, three-day tour is $390 per person.

Victoria Winery Tours, ph 9621 2089 - personalised and informative day tours to the Yarra Valley, Macedon and Mornington Peninsula wineries, service includes city hotel pick-up, tours depart daily at 9.30am and return at 4.30pm, $90 per person (cost includes lunch).

Yarra Bend Garden Tours, ph 9482 2344 - two-hour nature walks with a conservational bent through some of the city's plum bushland, tours start at the Victorian Indigenous Nurseries Cooperative (VINC) and finish at Studley Park Boathouse, $10 per person (concessions available).

Sport

Melburnians have taken to sport with gusto. This is hardly surprising when you consider they're beneficiaries of a fabulous spread of events - the AFL Grand Final, the Melbourne Cup, the Ford Australian Tennis Open and the Formula One Grand Prix to name just a few - throughout the year, that basic service at most major venues has, almost without exception, improved out of sight, and that an increasing number of column inches and TV programs dedicated to sport have now entered the fray. Never before have one citys sport's lovers been so well treated or so far ahead of the field.

For participants rather than spectators Melbourne also offers a range of activities such as golf, roller blading, cycling, boating, sailing and diving.

Australian Football League (AFL)

The Australian Football League ('Aussie Rules' to its followers, 'Aerial Ping-Pong' or a style of football played only because the populace is denied any better form of recreation to its detractors) dominates both Melbourne's sporting calendar and psyche. In fact its hard to imagine another city in the world where a sport so completely takes over. During the long winter months footballers with dicky knees and troublesome groins command front-page news, host TV game and fishing shows with all the aplomb of a Rob Lowe movie, or refer to each other as 'God' - all that sort of childish claptrap (Melburnians, if you hadn't already noticed, are all about creating celluloid paladins from their sportsfolk and papier-mâché castles of their football culture, even in its most unglamorous years).

Yet its success has been nothing short of remarkable. First played on the Victorian goldfields in the 1840s when Irish and English miners introduced Gaelic football to the colony, the game evolved in 1897 to become the Victorian Football League (VFL), then finally went national with the introduction of the AFL in 1990 (much to the chagrin of fanatical Victorians who were denied playing and watching it exclusively). Eleven teams now compete from Victoria, two from Western Australia, two from South Australia, and one each from New South Wales and Queensland, with moves afoot to also include Tasmania in the competition.

At its best AFL is an action-packed, fast-flowing game where players grab jaw-dropping marks, place deft kicks and give handballs to team mates up the ground, and boot with unerring accuracy for goal (a goal is worth six points, a miss or 'behind' to the left or right of the posts is awarded one point). But at its worst the game can degenerate into a series of 'ball ups', inconclusive wrestles at the centre square and the unedifying spectacle of players charging down referees when a dubious penalty is awarded against them.

The AFL competition concludes on the last day in September at the MCG (affectionately known as 'the Gee') where routinely huge crowds of 100,000 come to barrack for their favourite team.

Apart from the MCG, matches are also played at *Optus Park* (home of the Carlton Football Club), *Waverley Park* (St Kilda and Hawthorn), *Kardinia Park* (Geelong), *Victoria Park* (Collingwood) and the leagues worst ground, the perennially mud-caked *Western Oval* (Footscray). Plans are underway to build a $200 million 50,000-seater stadium (tentatively named the Victoria Stadium) to be located behind Spencer Street Station. Its state-of-the-art features will include great spectator amenities, a permanent roof and movable seating. Unfortunately construction of the facility will almost certainly sound the death knell for the popular Waverley Park.

Tickets can be bought at the grounds or from booking agencies, and usually cost from $12-$15 (reduced prices are available for children and concession cardholders).

Cricket

When Aussie Rules finishes, cricket takes over to hold Victorians in its thrall. The distinctive crack of leather against willow is best heard at the *MCG* where domestic and one day internationals, the Sheffield Shield

(Australias excellent national competition) and five-day test matches are played.

Victorian players who have excelled both at home and abroad include Shane Warne (peroxided leg spinner rightly regarded as the worlds' best), Dean Jones (ageing batsman extraordinaire), Damien Fleming (medium-pacer with a destructive outswinger), Brad Williams (tyro fast bowler on the brink of national selection who has been described as 'sending the ball down express post' but not always with the right address) and, if he ever gets another run in the state team, Merv Hughes (bristling fast bowler with the ample tum). Unfortunately the current Victorian team has, for the last season at least, played not with a bat or ball but with an air of resignation. Admission to major international matches ranges from $20-$40.

Horse Racing

The celebrated highlight of the Spring Racing Carnival (October 12-November 16) is the *Melbourne Cup*. Owners, trainers and jockeys from as far afield as New Zealand, Ireland, Hong Kong, Dubai and the USA come to compete in this 3200-metre event which began in 1861 and is now watched by a worldwide audience and has a prize-winning purse of $1.7 million. The horse race, run on grass at the attractive *Flemington Racecourse*, Epsom Road, ph 9371 7171, is always held on the first Tuesday in November (a Melbourne public holiday no less).

Cup Day is also a splendid opportunity for Melburnians to flaunt their finest hats and outfits on the Flemington lawns, mingle with celebrities among the bubbly and marquees, place a bet with colourful 'bookies' (who offer fixed odds on horses from both the members and public arenas) or drink prodigious quantities of alcohol in the 'Birdcage' car park (this long-standing tradition can cost up to $1000 for a patch of turf).

The PTC provides excellent service on Cup Day with trains leaving Flinders Street, Spencer Street and North Melbourne stations to Flemington Station every 10 minutes from 8.15am. From Flemington Station, city-bound trains leave every 10 minutes until 9.10pm. If race-goers desire a more fanciful entrance they can rent a chauffeured stretch limousine (Occasions Car Hire, ph 13

2121 at around $500 for the day), or be flown in by helicopter (Helicopter Service Australia, ph 9379 4500).

Punters who don't attend Cup Day at Flemington should be aware that the TAB computer has crashed not once but twice in the last four years (a horse race that stops a nation as well as technology!). Tens of thousands of Victorians - as well as interstate and overseas visitors - were therefore denied the chance of placing a bet at the nearest TAB. To avoid a similar scenario, pick your winners at least a day early when the computers are not so busy.

Other high-profile horse races are the *Caulfield Cup* (raced on 19 October) and the *WS Cox Plate* (26 October), named after the innovative club secretary William Samuel Cox, and always a good pointer of form leading up to the Melbourne Cup.

Popular racecourses apart from Flemington include: *Moonee Valley*, McPherson Street, Moonee Ponds, ph 93723 2222 - also the city's main venue for harness racing. *Caulfield*, Station Street, Caulfield, ph 9572 1111. *Sandown*, Princes Highway, Springvale, ph 9546 5288. There are also a number of tracks at various rural locations.

Tennis

The game of tennis, as we know it, was invented by the French (some among us are sorry that they ever thought of it). Its home in Melbourne is the *National Tennis Centre* (formerly known as Flinders Park) in Melbourne Park, Batman Avenue, ph 9286 1234. Opened in 1988, the $74-million complex has over 30 indoor/outdoor courts (including a centre court, capable of holding 16,000 spectators, with a high-tech 700-tonne retractable roof) as well as a giant media centre. Each year the National Tennis Centre hosts the *Ford Australian Open* over two weeks in January, and *Davis Cup* matches plus other championship tennis matches are also held there.

The Ford Australian Open is enormously popular, attracting over 350,000 spectators each year. Tickets are highly prized, and range from $20-$40 in the first week and up to $75 leading into the finals (family passes are available for $45). Watch out for Mark Phillippousis ('Scud'), the young bullet-serving behemoth from

Williamstown, to be among the front-runners.

Courts can be hired at the National Tennis Centre for around $15 per hour (expect to pay double that for indoor or floodlit courts) or the following centres:

Collingwood Indoor Tennis Centre, 100 Wellington Street, Collingwood, ph 9419 8911.

East Melbourne Tennis Centre, cnr Simpson and Albert Streets, East Melbourne, ph 9417 6511.

Albert Reserve Tennis Centre, cnr St Kilda Road and Hanna Street, South Melbourne, ph 9510 3311.

Soccer

Like AFL, soccer has an equally fanatical (though much smaller) following in Melbourne. Attracting the most sponsorship and support are the Melbourne Knights and South Melbourne, two of the most successful teams in the national competition and breeding grounds for a raft of Australia's greatest soccer talent. Other popular Victorian clubs include the Collingwood Warriors and the Gippsland Falcons.

Melbourne's soccer clubs - like those in Sydney, Adelaide and elsewhere - are predominantly ethnic-based. Matches are either white-hot affairs (especially those involving rival and interstate clubs) or tepid yawns (usually due to low spectator interest; administrators often blame poor crowd numbers on Greek weddings taking place on match day). Most major matches are played at *Olympic Park*, Swan Street, ph 9429 6288. Admission is around $10.

Basketball

Basketball, the game dominated by men with freakish physical attributes, is one of the fastest growing spectator sports in Australia (Victoria has over 50,000 registered basketball participants). Local teams such as the South-East Melbourne Magic and Melbourne Tigers usually compete in the best-of-three Grand Final for the National Basketball League (NBL) title. Showdowns before 15,000 spectators are regularly played at the *Glasshouse*, ph 9429 6288, and *National Tennis Centre* at Melbourne Park.

Formula One Grand Prix

Melbourne hosts a round of Formula One World

Championship racing each March. The four-day event attracts various car cognoscenti from Australia and around the world who come to watch piloted missiles doing laps around a rubber-coated, asphalt track at *Albert Park*. Other activities include support races, celebrity events, street parties, grand balls and the odd protest.

Tickets to the event range from $27 for the first day to $67 for day four (a four-day ticket is $120).

Melbourne's Formula One Grand Prix was voted the world's best course in 1996.

Golf

Oscar Wildes aphorism that 'golf is the ruin of a good walk' has not been heeded in Melbourne as it now boasts more golf courses than any other city in Australia. The city also has four of the Top 100 golf courses in the world including the *Royal Melbourne Golf Club*, ph 9589 6755, *Huntingdale Golf Club*, ph 9579 4622, and *Kingston Heath Golf Club*, ph 9551 1995. Unfortunately these glamorous and relatively flat sandbelt course are for members only but the general public can get in a round at the following:

Albert Park Public Golf Course, Queens Road, Elwood, ph 9510 5588.

Royal Park Public Golf Course, Popular Road, Parkville, ph 9387 3585.

Sandringham Golf Links, Cheltenham Road, Cheltenham, ph 9598 6755.

Yarra Bend Golf Course, Yarra Bend Road, Fairfield, ph 9481.

Malvern Valley Golf Course, Golfers Drive, East Malvern, ph 9563 1877.

Most of these courses have pro shops where you can hire clubs and buggies or pay for lessons. Bank on paying around $15-$20 for an 18-hole round.

Roller Blading

Roller blading is a popular activity in Melbourne, especially along St Kilda's bayside bike tracks. Skates and equipment can be hired at:

Bobs Boards and Blades, 17 Fitzroy St, St Kilda, ph 9537 2118.

Rock 'n Roll 'n Skate Hire, 11 Fitzroy Street, St Kilda, ph 9525 3434.

Apache Junction Skate Hire, 16 Marine Parade, St Kilda,

ph 9534 4006.

Prices are around $8 for the first hour, $7 for the second hour and $5 for every hour after that.

Pool and Snooker

Melbournes pool parlours include:

Cue, 277 Brunswick Street, Fitzroy - true tables, very friendly staff, food and beverage services.

Golden Triangle Snooker Centre, 1st Floor, 2 Walker St, Prahran -over 40 tables, food & beverage, coaching available.

The Master Billiard and Snooker Club, 150 Barkly Street, St Kilda - tables by the score, very popular.

Cycling

See under Bicycle in the Getting Around chapter.

Swimming

Melbourne's lack of world-class swimming beaches is more than compensated by its excellent man-made facilities. The best is the Melbourne City Baths, cnr Swanston and Victoria streets. This Italianate-style complex, with its distinctive red and cream brickwork, was constructed in 1903 and has swimming pools, squash courts, spas and saunas, plus an excellent gymnasium. It's open weekdays from 6am-10pm, & weekends from 8am-6pm.

The city has over 100 public pools, of every conceivable shape and design, including:

State Swimming Centre, Batman Avenue, City.

Fitzroy Swimming Pool, cnr Alexander Parade and Young Street, Fitzroy.

Carlton Baths Community Centre, 248 Rathdowne Street, Carlton.

Prahran Pool, 41 Essex Street, Prahran.

St Kilda Swim Centre, 97b Alma Road, St Kilda.

Harold Holt Swimming Centre (cheekily named after an ex-Australian Prime Minister who mysteriously drowned), cnr High and Edgar streets, Glen Iris.

Boating, Sailing and Fishing

Boats can be hired for fishing, sailing and generally tooling around at:

Studley Park Boathouse, Boathouse Road, Kew, ph 9853 1972.

Williamstown/Southgate Boat Hire, Parsons Marina, 34 The Strand, Williamstown, ph 9397 7312.

Keefers Boat Hire, Beach Road (opposite the Beaumaris Hotel), Beaumaris, ph 9589 3917.

Let's Go Fishing Charters, St Kilda Marina, ph 9568 5177.

Peter Dee's Boat Charter, Sandringham, ph 015 316 331.

If you want to learn to sail, take a navigation course, or crew a racing yacht try the following:

A Yachtmaster Sailing School, 56 Larnock St, Prahran, ph 9510 7469.

Jolly Roger School of Sailing and Boat Hire, Albert Park, Lake Aquatic Drive, South Melbourne, ph 9690 5862.

Royal Melbourne Yacht Squadron, Pier Road, St Kilda, ph 9525 5221.

Melbourne Sailing School, St Kilda Marina, 14 Reserve Road, Beaumaris, ph 9589 1433.

Sailboarding

Melbourne's bays offer great opportunities for sailboarding. Companies hiring boards and equipment include:

Repeat Performance Sailboards, 87 Ormond Road, Elwood, ph 9525 6475.

Sailboard HQ, 36 Jetty Road, Sandringham, ph 9598 2867.

Diving

A number of dive centres operate around the bay, including:

Melbourne Diving Services, ph 9459 4111.

Dolphin Discovery Tours, ph (018) 392 507.

Polperro Dolphin Swimming Tours, ph (018) 174 160.

Queenscliff Marine Discovery Centre, ph (052) 583 344.

Acknowledgements

I would like to thank the following people for their help and assistance in the preparation of this guidebook: Katie Cody for her countenance and words of advice; Darren Hopton for his keen photographic eye and production skills; the ever-resourceful Dave Collins who helped compile some useful and interesting information; and Danny Watson whose wherewithal made possible the writing of this book. Special thanks are also extended to Charles, Fay and the rest of the team at Little Hill Press.

About the Author

Stephen Townshend originally hails from New Zealand (somebody had to). He moved to Australia in the mid-1980s, living and revelling in Perth and Sydney before finally settling in Melbourne in 1994. He has worked as a journalist and editor in New Zealand, Australia and the USA, written articles for a number of newspapers including the *Sydney Morning Herald* and *The Age*, and published his own magazines. His hobbies cover a rather wide swathe but he is especially keen on politics, popular culture, the sciences, travel and the arts, and dining late into the night in his singlet and shorts.

In 1995 he researched, wrote and photographed the Little Hills Press Guide to Cuba before beginning work on this guide.

About the Photographer

Darren Hopton was raised in Portsmouth, England. He has visited numerous destinations in Europe and South-East Asia and, when not travelling, lives in Sydney where he works as a freelance photographer.

Index

Index to Maps

Another great travel title by
Little Hills Press

See our Home Page
http://www.littlehills.com

MELBOURNE CITY CENTRE

KEY

- **i** Information centre
- **+** Hospital
- *Pool* Swimming pool
- Railway
- ● *Central* Railway station
- Major road
- Other road
- Park
- Mall or public space
- Tram/Light rail route

NORTH MELBOURNE
to Airport

4 Flagstaff Gardens

Flagstaff Station

La Trobe

MELBOURNE

Spencer St Station

Crown Casino

SOUTH MELBOURNE

World Congress Centre 79

World Trade Centre 80 81

South Wharf Road
to Polly Woodside

Melbourne Exhibition 91